SECURITIES REGULATION IN JAPAN

SECURITIES REGULATION IN JAPAN

by
MISAO TATSUTA

UNIVERSITY OF WASHINGTON PRESS
Seattle and London

Originally published in 1970 by
UNIVERSITY OF TOKYO PRESS
UTP No. 3032–37033–5149
UNIVERSITY OF WASHINGTON PRESS edition, 1971
Library of Congress Catalog Card Number 77–165013

Printed in Japan

FOREWORD

In early 1966, I agreed to prepare a chapter on securities regulation for the forthcoming volume on business and private organization of the Encyclopedia of International and Comparative Law. At that time Professor Misao Tatsuta was in the United States with his family. I prevailed upon him to spend a summer in Berkeley and prepare a position paper on Securities Regulation in Japan to provide background for my broader study of securities regulation. The International Legal Studies Program of the University of California, School of Law, Berkeley financed this project.

I was extremely fortunate in having Professor Tatsuta undertake this study. He had spent a year in Berkeley studying American corporation law and securities regulation and therefore was thoroughly familiar with the most recent developments in the United States and in Japan. The result of his labors has produced an incisive and imaginative monograph on securities law in Japan. The study will be of immense value both to the novice and to the expert who wishes to obtain a greater knowledge of Japanese securities law. Its availability in English will open up to many foreigners the opportunity to learn something about the subject, despite their inability to read the Japanese language.

As Professor Tatsuta indicates, Professor Masahiro Kitazawa and Professor Akio Takeuchi, during later vistits to Berkeley, were kind enough to review his manuscript and add supplementary notes bringing the study up to date. Further revisions were made by the author prior to final publication.

This monograph continues the collaboration between Japanese scholars and the faculty of the University of California School of Law, Berkeley in the post-war period. The cooperation began in 1957–58 when Professor Kitazawa first visited the Berkeley Law School. I later had the good fortune of being invited to be a visiting Professor at Tokyo University in 1961 under the Fulbright Program where I worked closely with Professor Makoto Yazawa of the Faculty of Law as his closest colleague. I there met Professor Akio Takeuchi who spent the academic year in Berkeley in 1968–69. In the summer of 1969 I revisited Japan to participate in a seminar on the comparative study of U.S.-Japanese Securities Regulation sponsored by the Japan Securities Research Institute. It was then that I formed a warm friendship with Mr. Haruji Yoshida, President of the Institute, the sponsor of this publication. This visit afforded me the opportunity of again collaborating with Professor Yazawa and Professor Tatsuta, and renewing friendships with the Japanese scholars and experts on securities regulation.

I am confident that this monograph will be welcomed by all those who have an interest in the comparative study of securities regulation. I also hope that it will be a milestone in collaboration between Japanese and American legal scholars, and that it will be followed by similar efforts in the coming years. The University of California, School of Law, Berkeley is proud of the financial support which it gave to Professor Tatsuta and congratulates him upon the excellence of the study which he produced.

Richard W. Jennings
Coffroth Professor of Law

June, 1970
University of California
School of Law
Berkeley

ACKNOWLEDGMENTS

It was in the summer of 1966 that I wrote the original manuscript of this book thanks to the kind suggestion of Professor Richard W. Jennings of the University of California, School of Law, Berkeley. Through his favor, the study was financed by the International Legal Studies Program of the University of California, School of Law, Berkeley. My family and I are grateful to have enjoyed the summer at that memorable place, Berkeley.

After I had left there, Professor Masahiro Kitazawa of Nagoya University and Professor Akio Takeuchi of the University of Tokyo studied with Professor Jennings at Berkeley in 1967 and 1968, respectively. Both of these outstanding Japanese scholars took pains in writing notes to bring the paper up to date and to supplement its deficiencies. I made the most of their valuable notes in this book.

The original paper was written for the personal use of Professor Jennings and I never dreamed of its publication. Last summer, when he made his second visit to Japan to lead the seminar on comparative study of U.S.-Japanese securities regulation, he sounded out the Japan Securities Research Institute as to whether it would be interested in publishing the paper. Mr. Haruji Yoshida, President of the Institute, generously offered the Institute's sponsorship of the publication. Then came the kind arrangement by Professor Makoto Yazawa of the University of Tokyo, thanks to which the University of Tokyo Press agreed to publish this book.

I hope that this book will serve the promotion of comparative study of securities regulation. I am grateful to have this opportunity to return the kindness of the gentlemen and the institutions who have enabled this work to be published.

Misao Tatsuta

June, 1970
Faculty of Law
Kyoto University

CONTENTS

LIST OF ABBREVIATIONS

COMM. CODE	Commercial Code (*Shōhō*) (Law No. 48, 1899).
Corporate Reports Regulation	Regulations concerning balance sheet and income statement of stock corporations (*Kabushiki-gaisha no taishakutaishōhyō oyobi son'ekikeisansho ni kansuru kisoku*) (Ministry of Justice Rule No. 31, 1963).
Exchange Rule	Ministerial rule concerning securities exchanges (*Shōkentorihikisho ni kansuru shōrei*) (Ministry of Finance Rule No. 76, 1953).
Financial Statement Regulation	Regulations concerning the terms, form and method of preparing financial statements (*Zaimushohyō tō no yōgo, yōshiki oyobi sakusei-hōhō ni kansuru kisoku*) (Ministry of Finance Rule No. 59, 1963).
FUJITA	FUJITA, KUNINOSUKE, *Shōkentorihiki Seidoron* (Treatise on securities legislation), 16 SHŌKEN RIRON KŌZA, Tokyo, Daiyamond-sha (Daiyamond Publishing Co.), 1962.
Kakyū minshū	*Kakyūsaibansho minji saibanreishū* (Lower court reporter, civil cases)—reporting selected cases of high courts, district courts, and, rarely, summary courts.
Keishū	*Daishin'in keiji saibanreishū* (Great court of cassation reporter, criminal cases), 1922 through 1946. *Saikōsaibansho keiji saibanreishū* (Supreme court reporter, criminal cases), 1947 to present.
Margin Transaction Rule	Ministerial rule concerning transactions stipulated in article 49 of the Securities Exchange Law and bonds therefor (*Shōken-torihikihō dai yonjū-kyū-jō ni kiteisuru torihiki oyobi sono hoshōkin ni kansuru shōrei*) (Ministry of Finance Rule No. 75, 1953).
Minroku	*Daishin'in minji hanketsuroku* (Great court of cassation reporter, civil cases), 1895 through 1921.

Minshū	*Daishin'in minji saibanreishū* (Great court of cassation reporter, civil cases), 1922 through 1946. *Saikōsaibansho minji saibanreishū* (Supreme court reporter, civil cases), 1947 to present.
MOF ANN. REP.	MINISTRY OF FINANCE, SECURITIES DEPARTMENT, ANNUAL REPORT (*Ōkurashō shōkenkyoku nempō*).
ODA, MIWA & SUMI	ODA, HIROSHI, MIWA, TSUTOMU, AND SUMI, MASAYA, *Kaisei shōkentorihikihō, shōken tōshishintakuhō kaisetsu* (Explanation of amended Securities Exchange Law and securities investment trust law), Tokyo, K.K. Minato Shuppan Gassakusha (Minato Shuppan Gassakusha Publishing Co), 1954.
Proxy Regulation	Regulation concerning solicitation of proxies for listed stock (*Jōjō kabushiki no giketsuken no dairikōshi no kan'yū ni kansuru kisoku*) (Securities Exchange Commission Regulation No. 13, 1948).
Registration Rule	Ministerial rule concerning public offering or secondary distribution of securities (*Yūkashōken no boshū matawa uridashi no todokeide tou ni kansuru shōrei*) (Ministry of Finance Rule No. 74, 1953).
Securities Company Rule	Ministerial rule concerning securities companies (*Shōkengaisha ni kansuru shōrei*) (Ministry of Finance Rule No. 52, 1965).
SEL	Securities Exchange Law (*Shōkentorihikihō*) (Law No. 25, 1948).
SEL Enforcement Rule	Rule for enforcement of securities exchange law (*Shōkentorihikihō shikōrei*) (Cabinet Rule No. 321, 1965).
SITL	Securities Investment Trust Law (*Shōken tōshishintakuhō*) (Law No. 198, 1951).
Soundness Rule	Ministerial rule concerning standards of soundness for securities companies (*Shōkengaisha no kenzensei no junsoku tou ni kansuru shōrei* (Ministry of Finance Rule No. 60, 1965).

SUZUKI & KAWAMOTO — SUZUKI, TAKEO, AND KAWAMOTO, ICHIRŌ, *Shōkentorihikihō* (Securities exchange law), 53 HŌRITSUGAKU ZENSHŪ, Tokyo, Yūhikaku (Yūhikaku Publishing Co.), 1968.

INTRODUCTION

The Securities Market in Japan: Its Size

Current statistics show that as of 1968 more than 18 million stockholders held shares in corporations having stated capital of not less than 100 million yen.[1] Nearly 100 billion shares, worth approximately 13 trillion yen, were listed on securities exchanges in December 1968; listed corporations numbered 1,552[2] Total amount of equity capital raised by all corporations during that year was 561 billion yen ($1.6 billion), of which 319 billion yen was raised by listed corporations.[3]

In 1968, the eight securities exchanges recorded tradings of 65.6 billion shares (11.7 trillion yen in value: $32.5 billion); volume and value of daily trading averaged 217 million shares and 38.8 billion yen ($107.8 million), respectively.[4] The size of the exchange market is at present about one third that of the United States. Over-the-counter trading in stock is minimal compared with that in the United States, as will be explained later.[5]

Issuance of debt securities such as debentures and government bonds valued 1.3 trillion yen ($3.7 billion) during the 1968 fiscal year.[6] Tradings in debt securities amounted to 4.7 trillion yen ($13.1 billion) in 1968, most of which were made over the counter by financial institutions.[7]

The aggregate balance of investment trusts amounted to 888 billion yen ($2.5 billion) as of 1968; new funds established during that year totaled 443 billion yen ($1.2 billion)[8].

---

1. *Zenkoku Shōken Torihikisho, Kabushiki Bumpujōkyōchōsa* (*Shōwa yonjūsannendo*) (Securities exchanges in Japan, Survey of shareownership as of 1968), 5 (1970).
2. 1969 MOF Ann. Rep. Table 17 at 334.
3. 1969 MOF Ann. Rep. 69.
4. 1969 MOF Ann. Rep. Table 7 at 325.
5. *See* p. 82 *infra*.
6. 1969 MOF Ann. Rep. Table 40 at 76.
7. 1969 MOF Ann. Rep. 100.
8. 1969 MOF Ann. Rep. Table 33 at 355.

Extent of Securities Investment: Corporate Finance and the Capital Market

Judging from the above figures, Japan appears to have an active securities market of considerable size. People's capitalism in this country, however, has a much shorter history than in the United States. It was only after World War II that *zaibatsu* combines were dissolved and most of the leading corporations actually became public.[9] Before then, a large part of the shares in leading enterprises were in the hands of *zaibatsu* families and of holding companies under their control. During the Occupation, most of these shares, amounting to approximately 14 billion yen ($40 million), were transferred to special committees and later distributed to the public through the SCLC.[10] This provided a stimulus to the subsequent growth of the securities market.

The market has expanded drastically since then. Most people, however, still prefer indirect investment to direct: savings deposits with banks and post offices form the largest portion of pecuniary assets of individuals (44.3%), while investment in securities by individuals accounts for only 15.5 percent.[11]

On the other hand, the average ratio of equity capital to aggregate working capital of corporations is 17.5 percent; stock capital constitutes 9.5 percent only.[12] In other words, corporations depend largely upon borrowed capital. Such an arrangement, due partly to the tax system and to steadily increasing inflation, is far from ideal, and improvement has been urged.[13]

---

9. Bisson, Zaibatsu Dissolution in Japan (1954); Iyori, Antimonopoly Legislation in Japan (1969).

10. *Shōken Handobukku* (Securities handbook) 697–98 (Shōkenshijō Kenkyukai ed. 1959). "SCLC" stands for the "Securities Coordinating Liquidation Committee" (*Shōken shori chōsei kyōgikai*), established by the *Yūkashōken no shobun no chōsei tou ni kansuru hōritsu* (Law concerning coordination of liquidating securities) (Law No. 8, 1947).

11. 1969 MOF Ann. Rep. Table 107 at 127.

12. 1969 MOF Ann. Rep. Table 251 at 278. Both the equity capital ratio and stock capital ratio have been constantly decreasing.

13. Sōgōseisaku Kenkyūkai, *Nippon no Shōkenseisaku—Shihonshijō Taisaku eno Teigen* (Securities policy in Japan—Proposals for measures concerning capital market) (Tsuchiya and Takahashi ed. 1969); Sōgōseisaku Kenkyūkai, *Nippon no Kōshasaishijō—Kin'yū Seijōka no Ikkan toshite* (Debt securities market in Japan—For the sake of financial normalization) (Takahashi and Fukura ed. 1966).

Right Offerings

It is customary that Japanese corporations issue their additional capital stock to the existing shareholders——and at par value, no matter how much higher the market price of the stock may be than the par. In 1968, right offerings accounted for 98.4 percent in value of the total new issues of shares by listed corporations.[14]

The law does not compel an issuer to grant shareholders preemptive rights as to new issues. Unless the corporate charter specifically provides that the shareholders are entitled to new shares in proportion to their holdings, shareholders are given preemptive rights only when the board of directors decides to do so by a resolution as to the issuance of additional share capital.[15] Nevertheless, almost every corporation confers preemptive rights to the shareholders to subscribe shares at par value.

This custom dates back to pre-war times when all corporations, large and small, were closely held. From the viewpoint of the shareholders, corporations were nothing but their own private property; payment for capital stock meant transfer of money from one account to another within a single pocket. Public investors, i.e., outsiders whose shareholdings formed but a small portion even in big businesses, looked forward to windfall profits from premiums. Public anticipation of such lucrative new issues has been taken into consideration in determining the market price of stock.

It has been difficult for corporations to raise additional capital through issues to the public at large at current market price of the stock, despite the fact that those corporations are now publicly held. Shareholders have accused the management of depriving them of their " vested rights " as to the stock price whenever deviation from this custom is attempted.

This traditional tendency of right offerings has been an obstacle thwarting the development of the issuing market for capital stock. The situation, however, is gradually changing. Not a few issuers recently began to offer a part of their new issues to the public along with right offerings to the shareholders.[16]

---

14. 1969 MOF ANN. REP. 74.
15. COMM. CODE, art. 280–2 para. 1 item 5, para. 2.
16. *See* pp. 35–36 *infra.*

Characteristics from the Legal Viewpoint

Unitary Legislation Securities transactions in the United States are regulated both by state blue sky laws and by federal acts. The multiplicity of state laws makes it necessary to cope with the attempts by parties to evade strict regulation. The dualism of state and federal legislation necessitates clarification of the jurisdictional means, that is, " the use of the mails or any means or instrumentality of interstate commerce, or of any facility of any national securities exchange."[17] On the other hand, since Japan is a country with a unitary legal system, no such problem arises so long as transactions are made within its territory. Issuers who attempt to offer securities nationwide have only to register them with a single bureau, the Ministry of Finance.[18]

Administrative Body Federal securities regulation in the United States is administered by the Securities and Exchange Commission (SEC), an independent board composed of five commissioners appointed by the President by and with the advice and consent of the Senate.[19] A similar commission (*Shōken torihiki iinkai*) functioned in Japan from 1948 to 1952. Under the slogan of simplifying the administrative structure, however, this commission was abolished, and at present the Minister of Finance is in charge of regulating securities transactions. In the bureaucratic climate of Japan it might be difficult to create and maintain such an administrative board, especially because of its radical difference from traditional governmental organizations in the eyes of government officials.[20] The Ministry of Finance has a special section, the Department of Securities (*Shōken kyoku*), to administer securities regulation under the direction of the Finance Minister. Harmony with other financial policies may be better preserved using this department, but it may be less easy to take quick and drastic steps than with an independent agency.

---

17. *E.g.*, SECURITIES ACT OF 1933, sec. 5, 15 U.S.C.A. § 77e; SECURITIES EXCHANGE ACT OF 1934, sec. 9(a), 15 U.S.C.A. § 78i(a).

18. *See* pp. 43–48 *infra.*

19. SECURITIES EXCHANGE ACT OF 1934, sec. 4(a), 15 U.S.C.A. § 78d(a).

20. The securities industry favored the continuance of the commission. SUZUKI & KAWAMOTO 24. Several independent commissions were organized at the end of World War II, but the Fair Trade Commission is the only survivor.

Scarcity of Case Law We find a great number of judicial precedents relating to securities regulation as well as orders of the SEC published in releases, both of which are very helpful for studying securities regulation in the United States. On the contrary, there are only a small number of precedents in Japan, and no periodical reports of orders of the Finance Minister.[21] Japanese avoidance of litigation in preference to resolving disputes outside of court is not a specific phenomenon confined to the securities field.[22] In the commercial field this tendency appears even more clearly. Furthermore, since the people's capitalism developed only recently, a very small number of people were involved in securities investment; moreover, the nature of the transactions tended more to speculation than to real investment. Speculation was regarded as a kind of battle, the loser ascribing his losses to his own bad luck, or to miscalculation in selection of parties and in strategy. Although the number of investors has drastically increased in recent years, the number of judicial cases is still quite small. Therefore, we have to depend mainly on texts of laws, cabinet rules, ministerial rules, releases issued by the Department of Securities, and legal writings when we study securities regulation in Japan.

---

21. MOF ANN. REP. provides statistics about orders made by the Finance Minister, but we do not know the reasons for these orders.

22. Kawashima, Dispute Resolution in Contemporary Japan, in LAW IN JAPAN 41 *et seq* (VON MEHREN ED. 1963).

CHAPTER 1

Laws Applicable to Securities Transactions

1. Sources of Law

The main source of law relating to securities transaction is the Securities Exchange Law of 1948[1] promulgated after the model of federal securities acts of the United States, more specifically the Securities Act of 1933 and the Securities Exchange Act of 1934. The Securities Exchange Law embraces both securities registration and regulation of broker-dealers and securities exchanges.

Priority Among the Sources A transaction of securities consititutes a " commercial matter " (*shōji*) within the meaning of the Commercial Code, and the Securities Exchange Law is one of the special statutes of commerce. Therefore, laws applicable to securities transactions include, first, the Securities Exchange Law; second, the Commercial Code; third, the commercial customary law if there is no express provision in the above statutes; and finally, the Civil Code.[2] The law most closely related to securities transactions is the corporation law part of the Commerical Code.[3]

Rules and Releases There are a number of cabinet rules (*seirei*) and ministerial rules (*shōrei*) promulgated under the Securities Exchange Law,[4] and these rules are effective as supplementary law so long as they do not surpass the delegated authority, being the same as in the case of the SEC rules and

---

1. *Shōkentorihikihō* (Law No. 25, 1948). The Securities Exchange Law will be cited hereafter as " SEL."

2. COMM. CODE, art. 1.

3. COMM. CODE, BOOK II (arts. 52 through 500).

4. The rules and regulations promulgated by the Securities Exchange Commission prior to its dissolution in 1952 remain effective as cabinet or ministerial rules under the amended SEL. Supplementary Provisions to the SEL as amended in 1952 (Law No. 270, 1952), § 2.

regulations. The Ministry of Finance also issues numbers of releases (*tsūchō*) with regard to construction of the Securities Exchange Law and rules thereunder. These releases, however, do not constitute direct sources of law, but are merely helpful in revealing attitudes of the administrative body toward securities regulation.[5]

Self-Regulation Securities exchanges and securities firm associations have their own constitutions, rules and regulations. These self-regulatory stipulations concern primarily regulation of their member firms. But some of the regulations referring to transactions between members and their customers were held to constitute adhesive contracts (*yakkan; contrat d'adhesion*) binding customers irrespective of their knowledge of the provisions, or even the existence, of those regulations.[6] At least they may well constitute commercial custom by virtue of their existence in the securities field over a long period.[7]

---

5. The fact that the administrative body handles matters in accordance with releases does not indicate the existence of administrative customary law. SUZUKI & KAWAMOTO 40.

6. Nittō Sangyō K.K. v. Yamada, 58 *Saikōsaibansho Saibanshū* (*minji*) (Compilation of supreme court cases, civil) 513 (Sup. Ct., 3rd Petty Bench, Feb. 6, 1962); Takeda v. Kachō, 7 Kakyū minshū 2964 (Tokyo Dist. Ct., Oct. 23, 1956); Ozaki v. Yoshihara Shōhin K.K., 23 Minshū 336 (Sup. Ct., 1st Petty Bench, Feb. 13, 1969). The first two cases concern entrustment contract regulations (*jutaku keiyaku junsoku*) of a securities exchange, and the third relates to those of a commodity exchange. SUZUKI & KAWAMOTO 245; NISHIHARA, *Shōkōihō* (Law of commercial transactions) 273 (1962).

7. A difficult problem exists as to whether a transferee, a buyer of shares *cum* right, may recover from the transferor new shares, subscribed by the latter when the former did not request the issuer to record his name on the shareholder register, in exchange for the issuing price paid by the transferor. Regulations of securities firm associations provide expressly for the transferee's right to recover, the transferor's right to retain a certain percentage of the premium, and for procedures and a time limit for the transferee's request, e.g., Tokyo Association of Securities Firms, Uniform Practice Code (*Tōitsu kanshū kisoku*) No. 4 (1956). It is clear that these rules bind the member firms only. But it has been alleged that the contents of the rules form commercial custom, effective to persons other than the member firms. The Supreme Court denied this contention and held that a transferee could not recover from the transferor at all, on the ground of Commercial Code art. 206 para. 1. Matsuba v. K.K. Daiwa Ginkō *et al.*, 14 Minshū 2146 (Sup. Ct., 1st Petty Bench, Sept. 15, 1960), *affirming* 3 Kakyū minshū 1010 (Tokyo Dist. Ct., July 21, 1952). *Contra*, Nishihara, *Shitsunenkabu* (Shares failed to be registered), in 3 SHŌHO ENSHŪ 30 (SUZUKI AND ŌSUMI ED. 1963).

2. Legislative History Prior to 1945

Exchange Law of 1893 and Its Predecessors In the early years of the Meigi Restoration, the dawn of modern Japan, the government enacted several statutes concerning stock exchanges, the first of which was the Stock Transaction Ordinance of 1874.[8] While commodity exchanges, especially those of rice, had their origin in the eighteenth century and preceded their regulation, stock exchange legislation was enacted by the government at a time when collective transactions in securities were still premature, for the purpose of establishing a modern legal system comparable to that of civilized countries of the West. The number of stock corporations was so small that the early trade on stock exchanges consisted primarily of government bonds and silver.[9]

After several subsequent reforms, some of which never went into effect, the Exchange Law of 1893[10] was promulgated. This statute, in effect for fifty years, regulated not only stock exchanges but also commodity exchanges, as did Continental legislation. One of the peculiar features of this act is that it provided for exchanges to be organized as stock corporations in addition to membership organizations. While most commodity exchanges were formed as membership entities, every stock exchange, without exception, took the form of a stock corporation, to wit, the exchange was run as a business enterprise to raise profits and the contributors thereto were, or at least legally could be, different from those who traded on the exchange. Shares of stock in the stock exchange itself were listed and traded on the exchange, constituting the most popular brand traded in the largest volume.[11]

---

8. *Kabushiki Torihiki Jōrei* (1874). KOTANI, *Nippon Torihikisho Hōseishiron* (History of Japanese exchange legislation) (1947) is an extensive work on the legislative history of exchanges. A brief description can be found in SUZUKI & KAWAMOTO 16 *et seq.*

9. FUJITA 138. The Meigi government issued and delivered a large amount of bonds to ancien régime officials (mainly *samurai*); the number of such recipients exceeded 480,000. It was not until 1886 that the volume of shares traded on exchanges outnumbered that of government bonds. Noda, *Senzen Sengo no Shihonchikuseki to Shōken Kin'yū* (Capital accumulation and securities finance before and after the war), in 1 SHŌKEN KEIZAI KŌZA 52 (NAKAMURA AND OTHERS ED. 1968).

10. *Torihikishohō* (Law No. 5, 1893). Major amendments thereto were made in 1922.

11. An "exchange in the form of stock corporation" had been introduced by the Stock Exchange Ordinance (*Kabushiki torihikisho jōrei*) of 1878. One of the hotly disputed reform issues was the problem of whether or not an exchange should be a membership

Highly Speculative Nature of Exchanges Stock exchanges at that time were highly speculative and did not function well as a part of the capital-raising market. There were several reasons: leading corporations were closely held by *zaibatsu* partnerships and by their banks, and even after a part of their shares were distributed to the public, these shares were traded mainly over the counter.[12] Trading in shares issued by a stock exchange itself, as mentioned above, created an exchange market with speculative element.[13] Another factor is related to the methods of trading on an exchange market at the time.

The Exchange Law of 1893 authorized "time transactions" (*teiki torihiki* or *seisan torihiki; Termingeschäft; opération à terme*) as well as spot transactions. The former could be settled either by counter-sale and set-off or by actual delivery of stock certificates. On stock exchanges most trading took the form of time transactions and were settled by counter-sales. In other words, parties to such transactions hoped to obtain a balance between selling and purchase prices. Transactions with three different settlement dates were available for one brand of stock at the same time, i.e., transactions to be settled at the end of the current month, at the end of the next month, and at the end of the month after next.[14] In order to mitigate the speculative nature of stock exchanges, the so-called "short-term time transaction" (*tanki seisan torihiki*) was introduced, whereby parties were, as a rule, to settle the transaction on the next day. However, in most cases of short-term time transactions, settlements were carried over, thus rendering them also speculative.[15]

Exchange in the Form of Public Corporation In 1943, when the entire national economy was controlled by the government in order to cope with the critical situation arising from World War II, the Japan Securities Exchange Law[16] replaced all surviving stock exchanges with a single securities

---

organization. The statutes of 1874 and 1887, the latter being generally designated as the "*Bourse* Ordinance," authorized membership exchanges only. These statutes, however, proved ineffective.

12. SUZUKI & KAWAMOTO 18–19.

13. FUJITA 161–64.

14. This type of future transaction is quite common in the case of commodity exchanges even today. See, *Shōhintorihikishohō* (Commodity exchange law), art. 2 para. 4 (Law No. 239, 1950).

15. FUJITA 244.

16. *Nippon Shōken Torihikishohō* (Law No. 44, 1943).

exchange having the character of a quasi-public corporation.[17] The government made a contribution to the exchange, appointing officers and councilors. This act constitutes a landmark in that it abolished exchanges in the form of stock corporations which had been a problem for a long period, repealed at the same time trading in the stock of the exchanges themselves, and prohibited time transactions except at the markets of Tokyo and Osaka.[18]

3. Securities Exchange Law of 1948

Legislative Process The Japan Securities Exchange ceased its activities just before the end of the war, and the exchange was dissolved in 1947, when it appeared that the Occupation forces would not allow an exchange of such nature to run the securities market.[19]

In 1947 the Diet passed the Securities Exchange Law;[20] however, only the part concerning the Securities Exchange Commission was put into effect.[21] Since the 1947 act incorporated many traditional features, such as the "licensing" of broker-dealers and the lack of an independent administrative board like the SEC of the United States, the Occupation forces advised full amendments to the act along the lines of U. S. federal securities acts. Thus a new bill was prepared on the basis of a memorandum supplied by the Occupation forces and copying almost verbatim main provisions from the Securities Act of 1933 and the Securities Exchange Act of 1934 of the United States. This bill became the present act in April 1948 without detailed debates in the Diet due to the urgent demand to reopen stock exchanges and the unlikeliness of obtaining permission from the Occupation forces to change the bill. This new act came into force in May, July and November of that year depending on its several parts.[22]

---

17. Eleven stock exchanges were in operation at the time. All were transformed into branch floors of the Japan Securities Exchange, but three of them were later closed down.

18. FUJITA 148–50. This reform, however, did not mean that the stock market developed into a real investment capital market, but that speculation funds were excluded from the market in order to tighten wartime control. SUZUKI & KAWAMOTO 20.

19. FUJITA 149.

20. *Shōkentorihikihō* (Law No. 22, 1947).

21. This commission, however, was a mere advisory body, without any rule-making or administrative authority.

22. SUZUKI & KAWAMOTO 21; *Shōkentorihikihō Kenkyūkai* (Research group of securities regulation), *Shōtorihō Seitei no Keii* (Legislative process of SEL), IMBESUTOMENTO (Investment, a periodical published by the Osaka Securities Exchange), Nov.-Dec. 1961,

Gist of the Original SEL The Securities Exchange Law of 1948 introduced drastic changes in the securities regulation of Japan: the registration of securities;[23] the Securities Exchange Commission as an independent administrative board;[24] the registration of broker-dealers and securities exchanges instead of the former license system;[25] segregation of securities business from banking:[26] independent certified public accountants[27]——all such features were entirely unknown previously. Moreover, while the act itself said nothing about types of transactions on securities exchanges but authorized the exchanges to stipulate, all transactions were to be settled by actual delivery of stock certificates. Thus the time transaction (*seisan torihiki*) with its long history disappeared from the securities market of Japan, primarily due to the strong suggestion of the Occupation forces.[28]

Subsequent Amendments After its promulgation, the Securities Exchange Law of 1948 was modified by eighteen amendments, the most important of which include those passed in 1950, requiring financial statements to be made in accordance with the Ministry of Finance rule and making the texts more readable; 1952, which abolished the Securities Exchange Commission; 1953, subjecting securities exchanges to license instead of registration; 1955, which introduced the securities finance corporations; and 1965, which deserves special reference.

---

at 27 *et seq.*, especially Mr. Yamashita's speech, at 28–30. Mr. Yamashita was an official of the Ministry of Finance and later of the Securities Exchange Commission and was in charge of negotiating with the Occupation forces in drafting the bill.

23. SEL, Pt. II (arts. 3 through 27).

24. SEL, Pt. VII (arts. 165 through 181). Although identical in name (*Shōken torihiki iinkai*), the new commission was entirely different from that of 1947. The latter, however, existed for only four years.

25. SEL, arts. 28 through 40, arts. 81 through 83 and 85. The license system was revived later.

26. SEL, art. 65. This is one of the most controversial issues in Japan, especially with regard to the underwriting of corporate debentures.

27. *Cf.* SEL, art. 193. *Kōnin Kaikeishi-hō* (CPA law) (Law No. 103, 1948).

28. On April 20, 1949, the General Headquarters of the Occupation forces requested that the Japanese government adopt the "Three Principles Concerning Securities Transactions." The principles were: (1) each transaction on an exchange market should be recorded in chronological order; (2) members of an exchange should, as a rule, trade in listed securities on the exchange market; (3) future transactions should not be made. SUZUKI & KAWAMOTO 22; Hara, *Wagakuni Shōkentorihikisho no Kabushiki Torihikikōzō* (Structure of tradings in stock on securities exchanges in our country), in GENDAI TORIHIKISHORON (Contemporary exchanges) 56 (SUMINOE ED. 1969).

The 1965 amendment[29] relates to three major points. (1) The registration of broker-dealers is replaced by license. This represents a revival of pre-war practice, but the license is to be applied and granted depending upon the business or businesses in which the broker-dealer is engaged. Securities businesses are classified into four types: dealer's activity, broker's activity, underwriting, and arrangement for public offering and secondary distribution. (2) It introduces stricter regulatory provisions as to broker-dealers. In order for them to merge, transfer or dissolve business, or change their firm-names, amount of stated capital, methods of operation or offices, a permit must be obtained from the Minister of Finance. It also introduces special kinds of reserves which broker-dealers are required to accumulate. In addition, it prohibits officers and employees of broker-dealers from engaging in certain activities detrimental to investors or to the reputation of the securities industry. (3) It subjects registered representatives of broker-dealers to direct regulation by the Finance Minister and expressly provides that broker-dealers are liable for the conduct of their customer's men.[30]

This amendment, as we have seen above, concerns mainly broker-dealers, with the purpose of making their financial situations solid and ensuring appropriate business conduct. The Securities Counseling Commission (*Shōken torihiki shingikai*) has pointed out the need to reconsider the issuance and negotiation of securities, securities exchanges and securities finance. Accordingly, further amendments are expected in the near future.[31]

4. Corporation Law and Other Statutes

Japanese corporation law, like securities law, was also transformed from a Continental type to that modeled after Anglo-American law by the drastic amendment in 1950. Major subsequent amendments were added in 1962 and 1966, the former relating mainly to corporate accounting and the latter

---

29. Law No. 90, 1965.

30. Miyashita, *Shōtorihō Kaiseihōan no Yōten* (Summary of the bill amending the SEL), SHŌJI HŌMU KENKYŪ (No. 341) 2 (1965); SUZUKI & KAWAMOTO 25–26.

31. On May 6, 1969, the Securities Counseling Commission decided to establish a subcommittee to review the present securities regulation. Sakano, *Shōkentorihikihō no Mondaiten to sono Haikei* (Problems in securities regulation and their background), SHŌJI HŌMU KENKYŪ (No. 487) 2 (1969). Improvement of the disclosure system will be the first topic for study by the subcommittee.

concerned chiefly with transfer of stock and issuance of new shares. Another reform project is under way at present, focusing, among other aspects, on auditing.[32] So far as it is essential for understanding Japanese securities regulation, provisions of the Commercial Code will be described below.

Formation and Capital In order to form a stock corporation (*kabushiki-gaisha*), seven or more incorporators (*hokkinin*) must sign the charter (*teikan*).[33] No statutory limit is set as to the minimum amount of stated capital of a stock corporation; partly for this reason, there exist a large number of stock corporations of small size.[34] The so-called "authorized capital"

32. Tanabe, *Shōhō no Ichibu o Kaiseisuru Hōritsuan-yōkō ni tsuite* (Concerning the summary of the bill amending a part of the Commercial Code), SHŌJI HŌMU KENKYŪ (No. 517) 2 (1970).

33. COMM. CODE, arts. 165 and 166 para. 1.

34. It is not easy to ascertain the exact number of stock corporations. According to the statistics of the National Tax Bureau, the figures were as follows in 1961:

Amount of Stated Capital	Number of Corporations
less than 200,000 yen	7,082
200,000 yen or more	26,571
500,000 yen or more	69,392
1 million yen or more	162,208
5 million yen or more	25,730
10 million yen or more	13,828
50 million yen or more	2,310
100 million yen or more	2,425
1 billion yen or more	436
5 billion yen or more	123
total	310,205

Of the above total, 279,003 were family corporations (*dōzoku-gaisha*). From 1962 on, such classified figures have not been published.

On the other hand, more than twice as many stock corporations appear on the commercial registry. The following figures are those as of the end of 1965, including such corporations as were in the process of liquidation and probably even dormant corporations.

Amount of Stated Capital	Number of Corporations	%
less than 1 million yen	288,574	41.13
1 million yen or more	365,917	52.15
10 million yen or more	41,489	5.91
100 million yen or more	5,674	0.18
total	701,654	100.000

MIMURA, *Kaisei Kabushikigaishahō* (Amended corporation law) note 1 at 11–12 (1967).

The number of listed corporations was 1,552 at the end of 1968.

In some industrial fields, such as banking, insurance, trust and securities, regulatory statutes provide for the minimum amount of stated capital as a prerequisite for obtaining government license.

was introduced by the 1950 amendment. Not less than one fourth of the total number of shares stipulated by the charter to be issued must be " issued shares " : the board of directors has the power to issue the remainder by its resolution.[35]

Shares of Stock A stock corporation may issue preferred or deferred stock in addition to common stock, as well as non-voting, convertible or redeemable stock.[36] Both par-value and no-par-value shares may be issued.[37] A stock certificate may be either in register or bearer form, so far as the charter provides for the latter.[38] Despite the possibility for such wide variety, most shares in Japan are par-value, common stock in register form ; the number of other types of shares issued is negligible.[39]

Acquisition by a Corporation of Its Own Stock A corporation is prohibited from acquiring its own shares except in four limited cases, even

---

35. COMM. CODE, arts. 166 para. 2, 280–2 para. 1 and 347.

36. COMM. CODE, arts. 222 through 222–7, 242 para. 1. The number of non-voting stock shall not exceed one fourth of the total issued shares. COMM. CODE, art. 242 para. 2.

37. COMM. CODE, art. 199. Par value shall not be less than 500 yen. COMM. CODE, art. 202 para. 2. Corporations formed under pre-1950 law, however, may keep and issue 20 yen par-value shares. Supplementary Provisions to the 1950 Amendment, § 4 (Law No. 167, 1950). Most corporations issue shares of 50 yen par value. Since the general belief is that stock of lower par value is more marketable and has a relatively higher market price, corporations having stock of 500 yen par value seek to be merged into corporations having 50 yen par value stock—often dormant corporations appearing only on the registry —and to change the name of the merging corporation to that of the merged, immediately after consummating the merger. During the year 1968, mergers for this purpose accounted for 8 cases out of 247 mergers having stated capital of 50 million yen or more. *Kōsei-torihikiiinkai Nenjihōkoku* (*Shōwa yonjūyonen-ban*) (Annual report of the Fair Trade Commission) 49 (1969).

38. COMM. CODE, art. 227 para. 1. As will be explained later, there is no difference in method of transfer between register form and bearer form shares. *See* p. 95 *infra*.

39. Par-value stock cannot be issued at a discount. COMM. CODE, art. 202 para. 3. *Cf.*, section 57 of the British Companies Act of 1948. Where market price of stock is below the par, the corporation is forced to use no-par-value stock in order to raise additional capital funds. Most buyers prefer par-value to no-par-value stock, without any sustainable grounds. The legislature conceded to this irrational preference. COMM. CODE, art. 213, as amended in 1966, permits a holder of no-par-value shares to request the issuer to convert them into par-value shares, subject to a certain requirement with regard to the amount of stated capital.

when the price is paid out of earned surplus.[40] The prevailing view is that this prohibition extends to a subsidiary's acquisition of parent stock and to such acquisition as is made for its account under a name other than that of the issuer. On the other hand, the following acquisitions are not forbidden: gratis acquisition; acquisition by a trust company of its own shares as a trustee; and acquisition by a brokerage of its own shares for the account of its customer.

Subscription Warrant If a stock corporation decides, by means of a board of directors resolution concerning issuance of new shares, that preemptive right may be transferred, the corporation should issue subscription warrants (*shinkabu hikiukeken shōsho*) not later than two weeks before the stock payment date. The corporation may decide by the same resolution, however, that it shall issue such warrants only to those shareholders who request them. Transfer of preemptive right is made by delivery of the warrant. Where a holder has lost his warrants, he may subscribe for the new shares by means of a stock subscription form (*kabushiki mōshikomishō*); his subscription might be superseded, however, by later subscription made by means of the subscription warrant.[41]

These provisions were introduced in the 1966 amendment to the Commercial Code. Prior to the amendment, conflicting views were held as to whether a preemptive right was transferable under the Code. Thus no market for preemptive right developed, although some special statutes expressly provided for its transferability. Since the addition of the amendment, subscription warrants have been listed and traded on securities exchanges.[42]

---

40. COMM. CODE, art. 210. The four exemptions are: (1) where the acquisition is made for the purpose of stock redemption; (2) where the shares are acquired through merger or transfer of business as a whole; (3) where the acquisition is necessary in order to realize the corporation's rights; and (4) where a shareholder exercises his appraisal right. The corporation must dispose of such shares within a reasonable period of time. COMM. CODE, art. 211.

41. COMM. CODE, art. 280–2 para. 1 items 6 and 7, arts. 280–6–2 through 280–6–4.

42. The 1966 amendment in this respect, of course, benefits the Japanese investors. But the actual reason for this amendment was to enable foreign investors, especially American investors, to sell their stock subscription rights at a fair price by forming a market of stock subscription rights. Although art. 17–2 of the Law Concerning Foreign Investment (*Gaishi ni kansuru hōritsu*, Law No. 163, 1950) had already expressly recognized the transferability of subscription rights of foreign investors, such rights were suspected to be disposed of at an unfavorable price because no such market existed.

Other Statutes In related fields we find, among others, such laws as the Securities Investment Trust Law,[43] the Secured Debenture Trust Law,[44] the Corporate Reorganization Law,[45] and the Securities Transfer Tax Law,[46] most of which cannot be referred to in this brief outline. Japan has no counterparts to the Investment Advisors Act of 1940 and the Public Utility Holding Companies Act of 1935 of the United States.

---

43. *Shōken Tōshishintakuhō* (Law No. 198, 1951).

44. *Tampotsukishasai Shintakuhō* (Law No. 52, 1905). Unsecured debentures (notes) are regulated by COMM. CODE, arts. 296 through 341–7.

45. *Kaishakōseihō* (Law No. 172, 1952). This act was modeled after Chapter X of the U.S. Bankruptcy Act. Nakano, Japanese Corporate Reorganization, 8 OSAKA U. L. REV. 18–40 (1960).

46. *Yūkashōken Torihikizeihō* (Law No. 102, 1953).

CHAPTER 2

Securities: Definition and Exemptions

1. Definition of a Security

In General The Securities Exchange Law enumerates securities within the meaning of the law:[1] (1) national government bonds; (2) local government bonds; (3) notes issued by a corporation pursuant to a specific statute: (4) corporate debentures, secured or unsecured; (5) certificates of contribution issued by a corporation organized pursuant to a specific statute; (6) stock certificates or subscription warrants; (7) trust certificates for a securities investment trust or a loan trust; (8) certificates or instruments issued by a foreign nation or a foreign corporation and having the same nature as those stipulated in each of the preceding items; (9) other certificates or instruments designated by a cabinet rule. In addition, the law generally deems as a " security " a right to be represented in one of the foregoing securities, even when such security has not been issued.[2] As for item (9), no cabinet rule has designated such additional securities thus far.

Limited Enumeration There is no counterpart to the American passage " investment contract " or " any interest or instrument commonly known as a ' security.' " Such interest or instrument not enumerated in items (1) through (8) falls within the category of a " security " only when a cabinet rule specifically designates. In this respect the definition by the U. S. act[3]

---

1. SEL, art. 2 para. 1. Securities of items 1 through 3, 5 and 7 are exemptions to be discussed later. As to subscription warrants of item 6, *see* p. 15 *supra*.

2. SEL, art. 2 para 2. This is commonly called a " constructive security " (*minashi sōken*). Examples include registered bonds, governmental or corporate, without certificates, and shares of stock before the issuance of certificates.

3. SECURITIES ACT OF 1933, sec. 2(1), 15 U.S.C.A. § 77b(1).

is broader than that of Japanese law.[4] Sales with management agreement, co-ownership in an apartment building, or a country club membership, ——all regarded as a security in the United States,[5]——may not fall within the scope of the Securities Exchange Law. Fractional undivided interests in oil, gas or other mineral rights are seldom offered to the public in Japan, and the legislature did not consider it necessary to cover these interests. A voting trust is not popular in Japan and scholarly views are split with regard to its validity.[6] A share-interest or quota (*mochibun; Anteil*) in a partnership corporation (*gōmei-gaisha; offene Handeslgesellschaft*) or in a limited partnership corporation (*gōshi-gaisha*; *Kommanditgesellschaft*) is not a security within the meaning of the law.[7]

---

4. Yazawa, *Amerika ni okeru Kaishahō to Shōkentorihikihō* (Corporation law and securities regulation in America), SHŌJI HŌMU KENKYŪ (No. 49) 29 (1957). Some scholars interpret SEL, art 2 para. 1 as mere examples, not as limited enumeration. *See* Shōkentorihikihō Kenkyūkai, IMBESUTOMENTO, Jan.-Feb. 1962, at 125. It might be difficult, however, to generally include an instrument or contract beyond the statutory definition of a " security " which would be subject to administrative regulation as well as to civil and penal liabilities, without specific designation by a cabinet rule pursuant to item 9. This does not mean that each item need not be construed with reasonable elasticity.

5. SEC v. W. J. Howey Co., 328 U.S. 293 (1946); Sire Plan Portfolios, Inc. v. Carpentier, 8 Ill. App. 2d 354, 132 N.E. 2d 78 (1956); Silver Hills Country Club v. Sobieski, 55 Cal. 2d 811, 361 P. 2d 906 (1961).

6. The majority view is that a voting trust is valid so far as it is not used for an illegal purpose; this view presupposes that the trust is not confined to the voting right but extends to the stock itself. 2 ŌSUMI, *Zentei Kaishahōron* (Treatise on corporation law) 34–35 (rev. ed. 1959); 1 ISHII, *Kaishahō* (Corporation law), 248–49 (1967); 1 SEIJI TANAKA, *Kaishahō Shōron* (Details on corporation law) 386 (1967); Suzuki, *Kyōekiken no Honshitsu* (The essential nature of shareholders' rights of common interest), 62 HŌGAKU KYŌKAI ZASSHI 312 (1944); NISHIHARA, *Kaishahō* (Corporation law) 229 (2d ed. 1969); Ōmori, *Giketsuken* (Voting right), 3 KABUSHIKIGAISHAHŌ KŌZA 894 (TANAKA ED. 1956); HISHIDA, *Kabunushi no Gikentsukenkōshi to kaishashihai* (Shareholders' voting and corporate control) 183 (1960). The minority view regards a voting trust as illegal per se. MATSUDA, *Kabushikigaishahō no Riron* (Theory on stock corporation) 315 (1962); KAWAMURA, *Kabunushisōkai no Kenkyū* (Studies on shareholders' meetings), 202 (1937); Matsunami, *Mukimei Kabushiki* (Bearer form stock), 2 KABUSHIKIGAISHAHŌ KŌZA 590 (Tanaka ED. 1956). The writer concurs with the majority view. Note, SHŌJI HŌMU KENKYŪ (No. 429) 17 (1967).

7. Several years ago a smart fellow invented a method of collecting money from the public using legally permissible silent partnership (*tokumei kumiai*; *stille Gesellschaft*) contracts. COMM. CODE, arts. 535 through 542. His business, the *Hozen Keizai-kai*, and similar businesses prospered for a time by collecting large contributions from the public who believed them to be savings deposits, paying high interest. All of these organizations fell into bankruptcy and the " depositors " suffered great losses. After this

Interim Certificate There is no expression comparable to that found in the American act "temporay or interim certificate for . . . any of the foregoing."[8] Until several years ago it took considerable time to print stock certificates, and it was customary for a corporation to issue a receipt for stock payment. The receipt represented not a share ownership but a right to request delivery of stock certificates. It was transferred widely by way of endorsement or otherwise as a substitute for a stock certificate before issuance thereof. Courts admitted that a share ownership might be acquired by transfer of this receipt[9] and that the receipt fell within the category of valuable instrument in the Penal Code in connection with a forgery,[10] but denied that the Securities Exchange Law was applicable to the receipt.[11] Such a receipt, however, is nothing but an interim stock certificate in substance and should be defined as a "stock certificate" within the meaning of the law.[12]

2. Exempted Securities

Provisions on the registration and the prospectus are not applicable to: (1) national government bonds; (2) local government bonds; (3) notes issued by a corporation pursuant to a specific statute; (4) certificates of contribution issued by a corporation organized pursuant to a specific statute; (5) trust certificates for a securities investment trust or a loan trust;[13] (6) certificates or instruments issued by a foreign nation or a

---

catastrophe, the legislature enacted *Shusshi no Ukeire, Azukarikin oyobi Kinri tou no Torishimari tou ni kansuru Hōritsu* (Law concerning control of receiving contributions, deposited money and interests) (Law No. 195, 1954), instead of including such contracts within the definition of a security.

8. SECURITIES ACT OF 1933, sec. 2(1), 15 U.S.C.A. § 77b(1).

9. Minobe v. Ogiso, HANREI JIHŌ (No. 72) 18 (Tokyo High Ct., Nov. 30, 1955). The court relied on commercial custom.

10. Japan v. Azumai, 13 Keishū 3127 (Sup. Ct., 2d Petty Bench Dec. 4, 1959).

11. Morioka v. Okasan Shōken K.K., 7 Kakyū minshū 419 (Nagoya High Ct., Feb. 23, 1956).

12. SUZUKI & KAWAMOTO 35–36; YAMASHITA, *Kaisei shōkentorihikihō kaisetsu* (Explanation of amended securities exchange law) 29 (1948); Shōkentorihikihō Kenkyūkai, IMBESUTOMENTO, Jan.-Feb. 1962, at 125. A receipt for stock certificates submitted with the corporation in case of a merger, stock split or reverse stock split should be construed likewise. IMBESUTOMENTO, *ibid*, at 131.

13. SEL, art. 3 para. 1.

foreign corporation and having the same nature as the foregoing except those of (5);[13a] and (7) other securities designated by a cabinet rule.[14]

Corporate Debentures Much more important is the temporary exemption for secured corporate debentures and such corporate debentures as have statutory guaranty with respect to their preferred payment (except convertible debentures).[15] As a result of this exemption most of the corporate debentures in Japan need not be registered, leaving only the required registration of rarely issued convertible debentures and unsecured debentures. The reasons for this exemption are as follows: (1) such corporate debentures are held primarily by financial institutions which are capable of investigating the issuer's situations; (2) corporations issue a series of debentures at short intervals in such amounts as are expected to be sold out; (3) issuers have published periodic reports and disclosed financial information by means of registration statements as to issuance of new shares; and (4) there is less need than in the case of stock to have issuers disclose information about such debentures with fixed interests and secured payment.[16] The draftsmen themselves justified this exemption on the basis of the lack of trading market for corporate debentures, and they argued that this was why the exemption was made "for the time being."[17] Such logic is no longer persuasive. Seventeen years have elapsed since then. Issuers have come to regard this exemption as their vested right. In order to create an active market for debentures, abolition of this exemption is crucial.

National Government Bonds Until 1965 the Japanese government followed the policy of issuing long-term bonds only in limited cases.[18] Prime Minister Sato, however, abandoned this sound policy by issuing government bonds to cope with deficits in the national treasury. Greater amounts

---

13a. *See* p. 108 *infra.*

14. SEL, art. 3 para. 2; SEL Enforcement Rule, art. 2. The exemption stipulated in this rule concerns mainly post-war rehabilitation or disposition of securities.

15. Supplementary Provisions to the Amended SEL., § 7 (Law No. 142, 1953). Debentures issued by electric power corporations have statutory guaranty for preferred payment.

16. ODA, MIWA & SUMI 23–24.

17. ODA, MIWA & SUMI 24.

18. This policy was instituted on the basis of the recommendation made by Joseph Dodge, then president of the Detroit Bank, as a financial counselor for the Occupation forces in 1949.

of government bonds were issued through the securities market from 1966 on. Trading in national government bonds on securities exchanges was reopened in February 1966.

Special Bonds and Notes Among " notes issued by a corporation pursuant to a specific statute," financial notes (*kin'yū saiken*) and bonds guaranteed by the government (*seifu hoshō saiken*) deserve to be mentioned. " Financial notes " are issued by qualified financial institutions[19] in order to raise funds to be loaned by such institutions. Notification to the authorities is required for the issuance of these notes. Individuals are rather willing to purchase these notes partly because they are the intermediate form between direct and indirect investments. Bonds guaranteed by the government[20] may be issued under an approval by the authorities and within the limit stipulated by the Diet.

---

19. *Nippon Chōki Shinyō Ginkō* (Japan Long-Term Credit Bank, Inc.), *Nippon Kōgyō Ginkō* (Japan Industrial Bank, Inc.), *Nippon Fudōsan Ginkō* (Japan Real Estate Bank, Inc.), *Nōrin Chūō Kinko* (Central Agricultural Bank), *Shōkō Kumiai Chūō Kinko* (Central Bank for Commercial and Industrial Cooperative Associations), and *Tokyo Ginkō* (Bank of Tokyo).

20. Present issuers are: *Nippon Kokuyū Tetsudō* (Japan National Railways), *Nippon Denshin Denwa Kōsha* (Japan Telegraph and Telephone Corp.), *Nippon Jūtaku Kōdan* (Japan Housing Corp.), *Nippon Dōro Kōdan* (Japan Road Corp.), *Hokkaidō-Tōhoku Kaihatsu Kōko* (Hokkaidō-Tōhoku Exploitation Corp.), *Kōei Kigyō Kin'yū Kōko* (Finance Corporation for Public Enterprises), *Dengen Kaihatsu Kabushiki-gaisha* (Power Dam Developing Corp.), *Nippon Kōkū Kabushiki-gaisha* (Japan Airlines, Inc.), *Tōhoku Kaihatsu Kabushiki-gaisha* (Tōhoku Exploitation Corp.), *Chūshōkigyō Kin'yū Kōko* (Finance Corporation for Small Businesses), *Shuto Kōsokudōro Kōdan* (Tokyo Turnpike Corp.), *Mizushigen Kaihatsu Kōdan* (Water Resources Exploitation Corp.), *Hanshin Kōsokudōro Kōdan* (Hanshin Turnpike Corp.), *Sekiyushigen Kaihatsu Kabushiki-gaisha* (Petroleum Resources Exploitation Corp.), and *Nippon Kōkūkiseizō Kabushiki-gaisha* (Japan Aircraft Mfg. Corp.). The first two are listed on securities exchanges.

CHAPTER 3

Public Offerings and Secondary Distributions

1. Significance of Their Definition

The definitions of public offering (*boshū*) and secondary distribution (*uridashi*) of securities have great importance under the Securities Exchange Law because they are key concepts in determining the scope of substantial portions of the law. They have functions corresponding to those of a " sale " under the U. S. securities acts. It should be borne in mind that secondary distribution here denotes something slightly different from that used in the United States, as will be explained later.[1]

Registration of securities is necessary only where they are to be sold by way of public offering or secondary distribution.[2] A statutory prospectus need not be used when securities are sold except in the case of public offering or secondary distribution.[3] Periodic reports (*yūkashōken hōkokusho*) must be filed with the Finance Minister by the issuer of securities for which the registration has become effective.[4] In other words, those issuers whose securities have not been sold either through public offering or secondary distribution need not file periodic reports, the main contents thereof being comprised of financial statements in statutory form.[5]

Several other regulatory provisions are also applicable only to public offering and secondary distribution.[6]

---

1. *See* pp. 24–25 *infra.*

2. SEL, art. 4 para. 1 main clause. The proviso of the same paragraph stipulates small amount exemptions.

3. SEL, art. 13 para. 1, art. 15 para. 2 main clause.

4. SEL, art. 24 para. 1. The propriety of this linkage between initial and continuous disclosures is questioned *de lege ferenda.*

5. SEL, art. 193. *See also* p. 55 *infra.*

6. SEL, art. 191–3 and art. 191–4 (Prohibition from making representation to the effect that the security may be repurchased at or above the fixed price or that a minimal amount of income will be derived from the security, in cases of stock or the like). Here, however, the scope of secondary distribution is broader than elsewhere in that uniformity of selling terms is not essential. *See* p. 24 *infra.*

2. Public Offerings

The term " public offering " (*boshū*) is defined as " a solicitation as against unspecified many persons, with a uniform term, to acquire new securities to be issued."[7] Key words are " unspecified " (*futokutei*) and " many " (*tasū*). The uniformity of issuing terms is not peculiar to this context, but is a general rule whenever new shares are issued.[8]

Right Offerings Some writers argue that a right offering is an exempted transaction because the shareholders are " specified " persons.[9] But the prevailing view is that since shareholders change from time to time, they are " unspecified," and a right offering is not exempt from registration.[10]

---

7. SEL, art. 2 para. 3. Here we chose the English phrase " public offering " as an equivalent to *boshū*, which is technically defined by the statute as quoted in the text. The English term " public offering," however, is commonly translated into Japanese as *kōbo*. The term *kōbo* is identical with *boshū* when it is used in contradistinction to private offering (*shibo*). Frequently, however, *kōbo* is used as opposed to right offering; in this usage it is different from statutory *boshū* which may include right offering. To avoid confusion, we use the term " non-right offering " to indicate *kōbo* in the latter sense.

8. COMM. CODE, art. 280–3. Where both right and non-right offerings are carried out simultaneously, issuing terms of the former may differ from those of the latter. COMM. CODE, art. 280–3–3 para. 1. As explained previously, it is customary that right offerings are made at par value (*see* p. 3 *supra*), whereas in the case of non-right offerings the issuing price must be fair, i.e., reasonably related to the current market price. *Cf.* COMM. CODE, art. 280–11. Scholars hold conflicting views in their interpretation of the provision of Comm. Code, art. 280–3. The majority opinion is that the provision merely requires uniformity in determining the minimum issuing price and that amounts actually paid by individual subscribers may vary. *See*, Ōmori, in 5 *Chūshaku Kaishahō* (Commentaries on corporation law) 64 (ŌMORI AND YAZAWA ED. 1968). With regard to corporate debentures, it is expressly provided that an issuer may set a minimum issuing price. COMM. CODE, art. 301 para. 3. The uniformity mentioned here concerns the subscription price. With regard to the selling price of a stock subscribed and offered by an underwriter, the same problem arises as in the case of a secondary distribution (p. 24 *infra*).

9. Yoshida, *Yūkashōken Todokeideseido no Kaizen ni tsuite* (On improvement of the securities registration system), SHŌJI HŌMU KENKYŪ (No. 85) 2–4 (1958); Matsumoto, *Yūkashōken Todokeideseido no jakkan no Mondai* (Some problems on the securities registration system), 3 HITOTSUBASHI DAIGAKU KENKYŪ NEMPŌ: HŌGAKU KENKYŪ (Hitotsubashi U.L. Annual) 140 (1961).

10. Suzuki, *Shōkentorihikihō to Kabushikigaishahō* (Securities exchange law and stock corporation law), in 1 KABUSHIKIGAISHAHŌ KŌZA 366 (TANAKA ED. 1955); Yazawa, *Mokuromishoseido no Kaiseimondai* (Problems of improving the prospectus system), SHŌJI HŌMU KENKYŪ (No. 81) 3 (1958); Asaji, *Yūkashōken Todokeidesho ni kansuru nisan no Mondai* (A few problems concerning the registration statement), SHŌJI HŌMU KENKYŪ (No. 29) 4 (1956); Nojiri, *Shōken no Hakkō, Torihiki o meguru Hōritsumondai* (Legal problems concerning issuance and trading of securities), 33(2) HŌRITSU JIHŌ 167 (1961); Fukumitsu, in 5 *Chūshaku Kaishahō* (Commentaries on corporation law) 115 (ŌMORI AND YAZAWA ED. 1968).

The Ministry of Finance takes the latter view and requires registration for right offerings.[11] Likewise, offerings to the employees or to clients are subject to registration.[12]

Number of Offerees As for the numerical test, the Finance Ministry regards an offering to more than fifty persons as a public offering.[13] Compared with the SEC criterion of twenty-five persons,[14] the Japanese test is much less stringent, but in many cases this test is sufficient because most offerings are made to the existing shareholders. This being a rule-of-thumb criterion, in case of an offering to persons other than the shareholders, the authority may take other factors into consideration.

This test relates to the number of offerees, in other words, target persons of the solicitation, and not to the number of persons who have actually acquired the security.

3. Secondary Distributions

The term " secondary distribution " (*uridashi*) is defined as " an offer to sell, or a solicitation to offer to buy, issued securities, as against unspecified many persons with a uniform term."[15] Its only differentiation from a public offering is that a secondary distribution relates to issued securities. Since it is strictly prohibited for a corporation to acquire its own shares,[16] corporations do not usually hold a block of treasury stock. A secondary distribution, therefore, occurs when a large shareholder disposes of his shares through the market.

Uniform Term Unlike the case of public offerings, the phrase " with a uniform term " in the definition of a secondary distribution gives rise to a

---

11. Securities Exchange Commission Release No. 10 (June 30, 1948).

12. Release, *ibid*; Yazawa, *supra* note 10, at 4; FUJITA 35. *Cf.* SEC v. Ralston Purina Co., 346 U.S. 119 (1953).

13. Asaji, *Yūkashōken Todokeideseido to Kansashōmei* (Registration of securities and audit certification), SHŌJI HŌMU KENKYŪ (No. 135) 11 (1959). The department of the Finance Ministry concerned with these problems once expressed a view to this effect in the form of a newspaper reply in the *Nippon Keizai Shimbun* (Japan economic journal), Oct. 1, 1956.

14. General Counsel's Opinion, SEC Securities Act Release No. 285, Jan. 24, 1935.

15. SEL, art. 2 para. 4.

16. *See* p. 15 *supra*. Accordingly, there is little difference, as a matter of fact, between issued and outstanding shares under Japanese law.

difficult question. Some interpreters argue that disposal of shares by a large shareholder through a securities company " at the market " does not constitute a secondary distribution within the meaning of the law but represents a mere retail of securities which is not subject to the registration requirement, because sales prices vary from day to day and the transaction is not made " with a uniform term."[17] The more reasonable view might be that the foregoing example falls within the definition of a secondary distribution, because everyone has an opportunity to purchase the security " at the market," i.e., at the same price at one particular point in time, and this equality of opportunity meets the phrase " with a uniform term."[18]

Under Japanese law, where, unlike U. S. acts, the concept of " controlling person " is unknown and that of " underwriter " is less elastic, as will be discussed later, the former view would create broad leeway for the distribution of issued securities.[19] Moreover, where the duty to file periodic reports is made dependent upon registration of securities, as is the case under the present law, such leeway would result in lack of both initial and continuous disclosure of information about the security.

---

17. Shōkentorihikihō Kenkyūkai, IMBESUTOMENTO, May-June 1962, at 56–57.

18. *Ibid.*

19. It is a requirement that " offering price " (*uridashi kagaku*) be stated in Form II, a registration statement. Registration Rule, Form II, Item 10. This would tend to sustain the former view which contends that a uniform term means a fixed price. However, it may be possible to state " at the market " in the column of " offering price " in Form II.

CHAPTER 4

Small Issues and Private Offerings

1. Small Issues and Distributions

Borderline Amount Offerings of securities of small amount are exempt from the registration requirement under the Securities Exchange Law.[1] Unlike the American regulation,[2] however, Japanese law draws distinction between public offerings (*boshū*) of new securities and secondary distributions (*uridashi*) of issued securities in terms of minimum amount. If the aggregate par value of securities involved in a public offering is less than 50 million yen (approximately $140,000),[3] or if the aggregate par value of securities involved in a secondary distribution is less than 10 million yen (approximately $28,000), registration of such securities is not required.[4]

The rationale for this distinction is that, without the foregoing legislative precaution, the registration requirement might be evaded by splitting a new issue into several blocks and by subsequent secondary distributions on the part of the subscribers.[5] Here again, the problem may be ascribed to lack of the " controlling person " concept and to less elasticity in the " underwriter " definition. If the above-mentioned evasion can be prevented by including such transactions as a whole in the category of a public offering, then it would not be justified to draw a distinction between new securities and issued ones.

Adding Up In computing the amount of a public offering, the aggregate par value of securities involved in previous exempted public offerings commenced or consummated within one year prior to the commencement of

1. SEL, art. 4 para. 1 proviso.

2. SECURITIES ACT OF 1933, sec. 3(b), 15 U.S.C.A. § 77c(b); Regulation A.

3. No-par-value stock is computed by its issuing price. SEL, art. 4 para. 1 proviso. The same rule applies hereafter. Par-value securities, on the other hand, are computed by par value, and not by offering price as under the U.S. regulation.

4. Registration Rule, art. 1.

5. ODA, MIWA & SUMI 22.

the proposed public offering should be added, and if the total amount is not less than 50 million yen, the issuer is required to file a registration statement.[6] But with respect to a public offering the payment of which was consummated within one year preceding, the aggregate amount of par value of securities for which payment was not made need not be included in computing the total amount.[7]

In the case of secondary distribution, previous secondary distributions are not included in computing the amount. Before the 1953 amendment, not only previous secondary distributions but also previous public offerings made within the preceding year were to be included in computing the amount of the proposed secondary distribution.[8] It is not necessary, however, to include previous public offerings since an issuer cannot usually distribute its own issued shares due to the strict restriction on treasury stock.[9] On the other hand, abolishing the requirement to include previous secondary distributions opened the way for evasion of registration by dividing the offering into plural distributions of small amount,[10] because if prices or other terms vary, the distributions are not, by definition, parts of a single secondary distribution.[11]

Exception to Small Amount Exemptions The following securities are not exempt from registration regardless of the amount of the offering: (1) foreign corporate debentures; (2) stock certificates or subscription warrants issued by a foreign corporation; (3) trust certificates for a foreign securities investment trust or a foreign loan trust; (4) securities issued by a registrant to be sold by way of a public offering or a secondary distribution during the period in which a stop order regarding his previous registration statement is effective against him.[12]

2. Private Offerings

If an offering of securities is made otherwise than by public offering or secondary distribution, such transaction is also exempt from registration of

---

6. Registration Rule, art. 2; Ministry of Finance Release (*zōri*) No. 6162, July 30, 1962.
7. Release, *ibid.*
8. Securities Exchange Commission Rule No. 10, 1948, art. 4.
9. Comm. Code, art. 210. *See* note 40 p. 15 *supra*.
10. Matsumoto, *supra* note 9 p. 23, at 160.
11. This loophole may be closed, to some extent, by broad interpretation of the phrase "with a uniform term" in the definition of a secondary distribution. *See* p. 25 *supra*.
12. Registration Rule, art. 3.

securities and from requirement of statutory prospectus, no matter how large the amount may be.[13] American lawyers take into consideration several criteria for determining what constitutes a public offering;[14] a variety of factors should likewise be considered in determining what constitutes a private offering (*shibo*). Nevertheless, it seems that most attention has been paid to the definitions of public offering and secondary distribution, thus disregarding the investors' need for information.

A private offering is contradistinctive to a public offering and a secondary distribution in the Japanese sense of the terms. The statute does not use the term "private offering" but states negatively, "where a security is issued or sold otherwise than by way of public offering or secondary distribution."[15] As we have seen previously,[16] both a public offering and a secondary distribution are defined as an offer or solicitation toward "unspecified many persons"——not "unspecified *or* many persons." Theoretically, therefore, where offerees are either specified or in small number, a private offering occurs. Realistically, however, it is hardly conceivable that offerees are specified and many. Existing shareholders, employees and clients cannot be said to be "specified." It may be practical, then, to say that a private offering is an offering toward specified persons in small number.[17]

3. Filing of Notification

Where Necessary An issuer is required to file a notification statement (*yūkashōken tsūchisho*) with the Finance Minister regarding the securities to be offered in cases where: (1) a public offering or secondary distribution is exempt from registration on account of the amount of the offer (small issue and distribution), except in the case where the aggregate amount of the par value of the securities to be offered is not more than one million yen;[18] (2) the securities are offered otherwise than by way of a public offering or secondary distribution (private offering), and the aggregate amount of the par value of the securities to be offered exceeds fifty million yen.[19]

---

13. SEL, art. 4 para. 1 main clause, art. 13 para. 5.

14. Jennings and Marsh, Securities Regulation: Cases and Materials 368–71 (2d ed. 1968).

15. *E.g.*, SEL, art. 15 para. 3 item 2; Registration Rule, art. 8.

16. *See* pp. 23–24 *supra*.

17. A rule-of-thumb definition is fifty persons. *See* p. 24 *supra*.

18. SEL, art. 4 para. 3; Registration Rule, art. 4 para. 1.

The requirement of filing such a notification statement enables the government to check on whether the offering is truly exempt from the registration requirement.

Notification Form and Attached Documents The notification should be made using Form I and should be accompanied by: (1) the charter; (2) a certificate showing unanimous consent by the incorporators relating to the issuance of securities, or a copy of the minutes of the shareholders' or the board of directors' meeting at which the issuance was approved; and (3) the prospectus if such is to be used in connection with the offering.[20] If any information stated in the notification changes before the consummation of the offering, an amendment to the notification should be filed with the Finance Minister without delay.[21]

Form I to be used for notification is much simpler than Form II for registration. Financial statements are not required for Form I and items to be stated therein are as follows[22]:

(1) the purpose of the issuer; (2) the date on which the issuer was organized; (3) number of shares of stock and the amount of capital; (4) description of securities to be issued; (5) description of securities already issued; (6) plans of subscriptions and of public offering or secondary distribution; (7) amount of costs and proceeds; (8) purported use of proceeds; (9) plan of private offering.

Waiting Period In the case of small issues or distributions, a public offering or secondary distribution may be made only after expiration of five days beginning from the day after the acceptance of the notification by the Finance Minister.[23] There is no such waiting period for a private offering, and securities may be issued or sold on acceptance of the notification.[24]

19. Registration Rule, art. 8. It is doubtful whether this provision is valid, because the SEL provides for notification only in the case of small amount exemptions and does not refer to private offerings. Shōkentorihikihō Kenkyūkai, 22(3) IMBESUTOMENTO 48–49 (1969). Incidentally, in the United States no such filing as to a private offering is required with the SEC.

20. Registration Rule, arts. 4 and 8.

21. Registration Rule, art. 6.

22. Registration Rule, Form I.

23. Registration Rule, art. 5.

24. Securities Exchange Commission Release (*shōhatsu*) No. 73, June 24, 1949.

Chapter 5

Issuer and Underwriter

1. Coverage of the Regulation

The requirement of effective registration and use of a statutory prospectus is subject to several exemptions, two of which have already been mentioned: small amount exemptions and private offerings. Besides these, the registration and prospectus requirement is not applicable to: (1) transactions by any person other than an issuer, one who makes a secondary distribution, underwriter, or securities company; (2) transactions by an issuer or one who makes a secondary distribution otherwise than by way of a public offering or secondary distribution; (3) transactions by a securities company or by one who acted as an underwriter, after one year from the effective date of the registration of the security (excluding in the computation of such year any period during which a stop order is in effect, issued pursuant to the provision of article 10, paragraph 1), except transactions by a participant in the public offering or secondary distribution of securities underwritten by him; (4) transactions by a securities company executed upon a customer's order, ——excluding the solicitation of such orders.[1]

These exemptions, derived from the American model,[2] require a clear definition of terms such as "issuer." The term "securities company" will be explained later.[3] In this chapter we examine the meaning of "issuer," "one who makes a secondary distribution" and "underwriter."

2. Issuer and Secondary Distribution

The term "issuer" is defined as "any person who issues or proposes to issue any security."[4] No such modifications or specifications regarding

1. SEL, art. 15 para. 3. In addition, the prospectus requirement does not apply to transactions between securities companies. SEL, art. 15 para. 2 proviso.

2. Securities Act of 1933, sec. 4, 15 U.S.C.A. § 77d.

3. *See* p. 68 *infra*.

4. SEL, art. 2 para. 5.

certain types of securities as given in the American act are added,[5] perhaps because such securities are not common in Japan.

Lack of " Control " Concept The American act extends the concept of " issuer " to a person directly or indirectly controlling or controlled by the issuer, or a person under direct or indirect common control with the issuer, so that the underwriter concept may be amplified to this extent.[6] Such a definition operates favorably in two respects: (1) in checking evasion from registration in case of a distribution; (2) in imposing civil liabilities on underwriters in the broad sense.

Japanese law, however, does not have such amplification of the issuer concept. In the case of registration, this does not make much difference, because a secondary distribution itself is subject to the requirement of registration,[7] and a transaction by " one who makes a secondary distribution " is not exempt, no matter who he may be. The problem lies rather in noninclusion of previous secondary distributions in determining the amount of a secondary distribution, thus opening the way to evasion of registration by dividing the offering into small transactions with varied terms.[8]

With regard to civil liabilities, the Securities Exchange Law originally provided that not only a registrant and an underwriter but also a controlling person thereof were subject to such liabilities.[9] But the 1953 amendment released underwriters and persons in a control relationship with the issuer or underwriter from civil liabilities for misrepresentation in registration statements. Thus, at present, only the registrant, i.e., the issuer, is subject to such liabilities.[10] In this one respect, therefore, it is not so important under Japanese law as under American law to determine whether or not a person is an underwriter.

" One Who Makes a Secondary Distribution " This is a notion peculiar to Japanese law which distinguishes an offering of issued securities from that of new securities to be issued. American law may dispense with this concept by virtue of its broad definitions of an issuer and an underwriter.

---

5. *Cf.* Securities Act of 1933, sec. 2(4), 15 U.S.C.A. § 77b(4).
6. Securities Act of 1933, sec. 2 (11), 15 U.S.C.A. § 77b(11).
7. SEL, art. 4 para. 1.
8. *See* p. 25 *supra.*
9. SEL, art. 18 para. 1, art. 22 (before the 1953 amendment).
10. SEL, art. 18 para. 1. This may be one of the points to be examined in the coming SEL reform discussions. Kitsukawa, Disclosure *Seido* (Disclosure system), Shōji Hōmu Kenkyū (No. 472) 19 (1969).

It is not easy to determine who "one who makes a secondary distribution" is. There are two possibilities.[11] One is that the term applies to a person who has been a large shareholder and is about to dispose of all or a part of his shares by means of a secondary distribution, i.e., through the market. Another view is that the term refers to a person who actually distributes securities to the public: where a securities company acquires a block of shares from a large shareholder for the purpose of resale to unspecified many persons, the securities company, not the large shareholder, is "one who makes a secondary distribution."

According to the former view, which the writer considers the more reasonable, the concept "one who makes a secondary distribution" corresponds to that of a "controlling person" under American law. On the other hand, according to the latter explanation, the term "one who makes a secondary distribution" substitutes for that of an underwriter, in connection with offerings of issued securities.

This conflict of interpretations relates to the problem of whether there can be an underwriting of issued securities under Japanese law, as will be seen later.[12] Apart from this, the provision for the exemption of "transactions by . . . 'one who makes a secondary distribution' otherwise than by way of . . . secondary distribution,"[13] makes no sense according to the latter view, which construes the term "one who makes a secondary distribution" as referring to a person who actually distributes securities to the public. According to the former explanation, on the other hand, the abovementioned exemption applies to transactions between a large shareholder and an underwriter or underwriters.

3. Underwriter

Definition The Securities Exchange Law defines only the term "underwriter," but not that of underwriting itself,[14] which of course can be deter-

---

11. Shōkentorihikihō Kenkyūkai, IMBESUTOMENTO, Mar.-April 1962, at 133–38.

12. *See* p. 33 *infra.*

13. SEL, art. 15 para. 3 item 2.

14. SEL, art. 2 para. 6. *See also*, SECURITIES ACT OF 1933, sec. 2(11), 15 U.S.C.A. § 77b(11).

Hikiuke in Japanese means both "underwriting" and "subscription." Where it is difficult to differentiate in context, distinction is often made by defining "*hikiuke* within the meaning of the Commercial Code" (subscription) and "*hikiuke* within the meaning of the Securities Exchange Law" (underwriting).

mined from the definition of the former. The term underwriter is defined as " any person who, in connection with an issuance of a security and for a commission, reward or other consideration in excess of the usual distributor's commission, purchases from an issuer, with a view to distribute, all or a part of the securities, or contracts with an issuer to purchase the unsold part of the security, or makes arrangements on behalf of an issuer for a public offering or secondary distribution of a security, or participates directly or indirectly in a public offering or secondary distribution of a security."

By this definition and as a result of the lack of amplification of the " issuer " concept,[15] underwriting may be confined to that which concerns an issuance of a security, and underwriting in connection with a secondary distribution may be excluded.[16] This, however, cannot be legislative intent, because the law itself refers to a " secondary distribution " when it defines the underwriter, notwithstanding the limiting phrase " in connection with an issuance of a security."[17]

Investment Intent When a person acquires from an issuer, with a view to distribute, all or a part of the securities in an issue, then that person is an underwriter if he receives an underwriting commission.[18] Without such commission he is not an underwriter, but he cannot distribute the securities until a registration becomes effective, if the securities have not been registered at the time of their issuance, such as in case of a private offering. It might possibly happen that a few persons subscribe to shares with a view to distribute them (thus under the guise of a private placement), and sell them separately each in the amount of less than 10 million yen (thus evading the registration requirement in connection with a secondary distributions). In such a case we should look to the substance of the whole transaction and

---

15. *See* p. 31 *supra*.

16. SUZUKI & KAWAMOTO 52.

17. FUJITA 31 ; YAMASHITA, *Kaisei Shōkentorihikihō Kaisetsu* (Explanation of amended securities exchange law) 14 (1948). The Securities Investment Trust Law (Law No. 198, 1951), art. 16 para. 2 defines the term " underwriting of a security " as expressly including an underwriting in connection with a secondary distribution. Furthermore, a cabinet rule and a ministerial rule under the SEL presuppose the inclusion of this type of transaction, for they refer not only to an issuer but also to an " owner " of securities as a counter party to an underwriting contract in discussing the term " managing underwriter." SEL Enforcement Rule, art. 3 para. 3 ; Securities Company Rule, art. 2. SUZUKI & KAWAMOTO *id.*, however, argues that the definition under the Securities Investment Trust Law cannot be relied on under the SEL.

18. SEL, art. 2 para. 6. *See also* p. 36 *infra*.

require registration at the time of the issuance if the aggregate amount exceeds 50 million yen, regarding it as a public offering.[19]

Underwriting Commission The provision defining the term " underwriter " can be construed in two ways: (1) the phrase " for a commision, reward or other consideration in excess of the usual distributor's commission " qualifies only a " person who . . . participates directly or indirectly in a public offering or secondary distribution of a security "; or (2) the said phrase covers the whole sentence, including " person who . . . purchases from an issuer, with a view to distribute, all or a part of the securities," as translated above at the beginning of this subchapter.

The legislative intent was probably the former. We can deduce this on the basis of at least two considerations: the Securities Exchange Law in its original version imposed liabilities for misrepresentation in a registration statement upon underwriters as well as upon the issuer[20]; the law refers to underwriters as well as to securities companies,[21] which presupposes the existence of an underwriter who is not a securities company.

As a matter of fact, however, especially after the 1953 amendment deleting underwriters' liability with respect to registration statements, it is hardly conceivable that an underwriter not be a securities company.[22] Japanese law, which contains the unique concept of " one who makes a secondary distribution," should be re-examined in terms of definitions central to its basic philosophy.

4. Underwriting of Capital Stock

Due to the prevalence of right offerings, most of the capital stock of Japa-

---

19. *Cf.* SUZUKI & KAWAMOTO 52–53; Gilligan, Will & Co. v. SEC, 267 F. 2d 461 (2d Cir. 1959), *cert. denied* 361 U.S. 896 (1959). Such a case has not arisen yet in Japan.

20. SEL, art. 18 para. 1 item 5 (before the 1953 amendment).

21. SEL, art. 15 para. 3 items 1 and 3, art. 191–2.

22. By definition, one who engages in underwriting as a business is a securities firm, which must be a licensed stock corporation. SEL, art. 2 paras. 8 and 9, art. 28. The term " underwriting," which forms part of the definition of a securities company, does not correspond to the term " underwriter." In connection with the former, " an arrangement for a public offering or secondary distribution " (similar to " best effort selling ") is distinguished from an underwriting, whereas such arrangement is included in the definition of an underwriter. SEL, art. 2 para. 6, para. 8 items 4 and 6. SUZUKI & KAWAMOTO 51. This dichotomy causes unnecessary complexity, as the underwriter concept does not serve to extend strict liability.

nese corporations is acquired by existing shareholders directly from the issuers, thus eliminating the participation of underwriters.[23]

Going Public There are some cases, however, where issuing corporations need the help of underwriters. When a closely held corporation wishes to go public, it offers the additional capital stock to the public, or its controlling shareholders distribute a part of their holdings through underwriters. This holds true particularly when a company attempts to become a listed corporation, since share ownership must represent a certain degree of dispersion in order to meet the listing standard of securities exchanges. In 1961, when three major securities exchanges extended their market by establishing "Floor Section II,"[24] a number of corporations of medium size were involved in this "go-public" movement.

Stand-by and Fractional Shares In the case of right offerings, a portion of the new issue may remain unsubscribed for a variety of reasons, or the total of fractional shares may be of substantial volume. Many large corporations offer these shares to the public through underwriters.[25]

Purchase-Underwriting (*kaitori hikiuke*) Moreover, not a few corporations have come to realize the disadvantage of right offerings at par value, i.e., the inability to obtain premiums otherwise available when the market price is much higher than the par value of the stock——and have come to take gradual steps toward non-right offerings at the market price. These corporations allot a large part of the new issue (say, nine-tenths) to their shareholders at par value and offer the rest (one-tenth) to the public at the market

23. After World War II only a few big corporations were established. In most cases, virtually all shares of stock issued at the time of a corporation's formation are subscribed by its incorporators, who usually transfer afterwards all or a part of their holdings to private parties, not via the securities market, or sell the shares through broker-dealers bit by bit. It is true that incorporators prefer to establish a corporation by public offering (*boshū setsuritsu*; *Stufengründung*) rather than by exclusive subscription (*hokki setsuritsu*; *Simultangründung*) which is subject to court control (COMM. CODE, art. 173); but those subscribers other than incorporators sought merely for the purpose of complying with the formality of *boshū setsuritsu* are mostly nominees or incorporators' intimate friends. Thus even in this case there is no need for the services of an underwriter.

24. *See* p. 82 *infra*.

25. The preemptive right of shareholders does not extend to fractional shares. COMM. CODE, art. 280–4 para. 1 proviso. It is customary for the issuing corporation to dispose of the aggregate of fractional shares on the securities market at the market value and distribute the proceeds to shareholders in proportion to their fractional share interests.

price through underwriters. The offer to the public is usually carried out in the following manner, commonly termed as "purchase-underwriting" (*kaitori hikiuke*). An underwriter (or underwriters) makes an agreement with the issuer prior to the issuance of stock to the effect that he will subscribe a certain portion of the new issue and will sell the shares for commission to the public at the same price he pays the issuer. The underwriter offers the shares to the public and concludes a sales contract with those who wish to buy the shares, receiving prior payment of the purchase price.[26] The sales period usually terminates a week before the date on which the underwriter is to pay for the stock. After obtaining stock certificates from the issuer, the underwriter transfers the stock to the purchasers.[27]

This method of underwriting is said to have originated around 1948 and flourished as the most convenient way for issuers to offer their stock to the public. But in 1961 a shareholder brought actions against several issuing corporations to nullify issuance of new shares,[28] alleging that in giving preemptive rights to new shares to persons other than the shareholders, a shareholder approval by special resolution should be obtained,[29] and that the allotment of shares to underwriters pursuant to the "purchase-underwriting" agreement without shareholder approval would be violative of this provision. In 1962 and 1963 a series of judgments were rendered by lower courts, all in favor of the defendants (issuing corporations) on the ground that such an alleged defect in the process of issuing new stock could not be argued after the consummation of the issuance, or that a resolution by the board of directors validated the issuance despite the lack of shareholder approval.[30] The Supreme Court affirmed these decisions in 1965.[31] But several of these cases, especially the first,

26. Purchasers are asked to give a "deposit" or "earnest" (*mōshikomi shōkokin*), but it is actually the full amount of the purchase price.

27. Thus the underwriter does not have to collect stock subscription forms with statutory requirements from the public investors, and the issuer is freed from the trouble of making stock certificates with names of the public investors thereon.

28. COMM. CODE, art. 280–15.

29. COMM. CODE, art. 280–2 para. 2 (before the 1966 amendment). At that time there was a concept "preemptive right given to third parties."

30. Nakajima v. Tokyo Shibaura Denki K.K., 13 Kakyū minshū 2473 (Yokohama Dist. Ct., Dec. 17, 1962); Nakajima v. Shin'etsu Kagaku Kōgyō K.K., 14 Kakyū minshū 178 (Tokyo Dist. Ct., Feb. 8, 1963); Nakajima v. Taisei Kensetsu K.K., HANREI JIHŌ (No. 324) 6 (Tokyo Dist. Ct., Feb. 8, 1963); Nakajima v. Kisha Seizō K.K., 15 Kakyū minshū 1029 (Tokyo High Ct., May 6, 1964).

31. Nakajima v. Kubota Tekkō K.K., 19 Minshū 1745 (Sup. Ct., 2d Petty Bench. Oct. 8, 1965), *affirming* 17 Kōsai minshū 248 (Osaka High Ct., June 11, 1964).

admitted in dictum illegality of omitting the shareholder approval, and shocked corporations with the possibility that courts might enjoin the process.[32]

These cases aroused a number of comments in the academic sphere. Although some scholars argued that a "purchase-underwriting" would be illegal without proper shareholder approval, the majority view was that a special resolution by shareholder meeting would not be necessary so long as the price was reasonable.[33]

Amended in 1966, the Commercial Code now provides that in order to issue new shares to a person other than the shareholders at a favorable price, shareholder approval by special resolution must be obtained after disclosing before the meeting the reason for the issuance.[34] This amendment, proposed and requested by corporations, has cleared up the controversy over "purchase-underwriting."[35]

Another problem regarding "purchase-underwriting" concerns the registration requirement. It is obvious that in this case securities companies subscribe to shares "with a view to distribute" them, and that trans-

---

32. Nakajima v. Tokyo Shibaura Denki K.K., *supra* note 30. Another reason why this case caused a sensation was that the defendant was Toshiba Electric Co., one of Japan's biggest enterprises with approximately 300,000 shareholders. Nakajima v. Kisha Seizō K.K., *supra* note 30, and Osaka High Ct. decision of Nakajima v. Kubota Tekkō K.K., *supra* note 31, took the same view.

33. *E.g.*, Suzuki, *Kaitori-hikiuke to Shōhō dai Nihyaku-hachijūjo no ni dai ni-kō* (Purchase-underwriting and the Commercial Code art. 280–2 para. 2), SHŌJI HŌMU KENKYŪ (No. 268) 2 (1963); Ōsumi, *Tokyō Chisai no Hanketsu to Kaitori-hikiuke* (The judgment of Tokyo District Court and purchase-underwriting), SHŌJI HŌMU KENKYŪ (No. 271) 2 (1963).

34. COMM. CODE, art. 280–2 para. 2 (as amended in 1966). Thus the peculiar notion "preemptive right given to third parties" was discarded. The amended provision looks merely to the issuing price.

35. In 1962, all public offerings totaling 596 cases were made by purchase-underwriting (*kaitori hikiuke*) by the security companies. But with the impact of Nakajima v. Tokyo Shibaura Denki K.K., *supra* note 30 (Dec. 17, 1962), "purchase-underwriting" sharply decreased to 136 in 1963, 26 in 1964, and 0 in 1965, and in its place "stand-by" underwriting (*zangaku hikiuke*) was used. However, since the 1966 amendment of the Commercial Code, "purchase-underwriting" has again become the method of non-right offering. Even when making "purchase-underwriting" offerings, issuing corporations often give their existing shareholders the right to buy new shares on the pro-rata basis from underwriters at the same price they pay to the issuer (*kabunushi yūsenbonyū*). In this case, at least economically, shareholders have an indirect preemptive right, which is regarded as a kind of preemptive right in the German Stock Corporation Law, art. 186 para. 5.

actions by securities companies are not exempt.[36] However, since Japanese law distinguishes public offerings (50 million yen or less exempted) from secondary distributions (10 million yen or less exempted), it is doubtful whether a registration statement for a public offering or that for a secondary distribution should be filed. It is argued that the securities company which has made a "purchase-underwriting" stands on equal status with other subscribers; therefore, registration is necessary with regard to the subsequent distribution.[37] This argument overlooks the substance of the transaction, that in the case of a "purchase-underwriting", offers to buy are to be made in the same period as subscriptions are to be made. The Ministry of Finance also handles this kind of transaction as a public offering.[38]

5. Underwriting of Debt Securities

It may be appropriate to describe the process of underwriting secured corporate debentures which constitute the predominant type of long-term debts. Indeed all these securities, except some types of government bonds, are underwritten and distributed in like manner. And so long as corporate debentures issued within Japanese territory are concerned, unsecured debentures (notes) are quite rare.

Underwriting Process Most underwriting contracts for corporate debentures are so-called "stand-by" agreements; that is, underwriters sell the debentures for the issuer and purchase the unsold part thereof.[39] In most cases, at the time of every issue the same securities companies form an underwriting syndicate. One of the "Big Four"[40] negotiates with the issuer as a managing underwriter, and the "Big Four" agree to sell eighty

---

36. SEL, art. 15 para. 3 item 1.

37. FUJITA 36; *cf.* Horikawa, *Shōhōjō no Hikiuke to Shōtorihōjō no Hikiuke* (*Hikiuke* under the Commercial Code and that under the Securities Exchange Law), SHŌJI HŌMU KENKYŪ (No. 37) 3 (1957); Yoshizumi, *Kōbo oyobi Hikiuke ni kansuru jakkan no Oboegaki* (Some notes on public offering and underwriting), SHŌJI HŌMU KENKYŪ (No. 53) 10 (1957).

38. Takenaka, *Kabushiki Hikiuke-gyōmu no Genjō to Mondaiten* (Stock underwriting business: its situation and problems), KAIHŌ (No.97) 72 (Tokyo Kabushiki Konwakai, 1962).

39. ŌTORI, *Shasaihō* (Law of corporate debentures) 114–19 (1958); FUJITA 92; Shōkentorihikihō Kenkyūkai, IMBESUTOMENTO, July-Aug. 1963, at 84 *et seq.*

40. Nomura Securities Co., Nikko Securities Co., Daiwa Securities Co., and Yamaichi Securities Co.

percent of the issue.[41] The rest is allotted to other securities companies qualified to act as underwriters.[42] The "Big Four" are responsible for purchasing the unsold portion of the issue underwritten by the syndicate. In reality, however, debentures seldom remain unsold for the reason described below.

Long-term corporate debentures are purchased chiefly by financial institutions such as banks, trust companies, insurance companies or the like and a very small portion is acquired by individual investors.[43] Even today financial institutions purchase more than eighty percent of the total issue of corporate debentures.[44] In order to cope with the general shortage of money in the financial market, the central bank (*Nippon Ginkō*), with the advice of the Finance Ministry, controls the amount and terms of bond issues by means of its influence on banks. Banks and underwriters meet every month to determine the aggregate amount, allotting the sum to corporations wishing to issue debentures.[45]

Segregation of Banking and Securities Businesses In pre-war days banks themselves formed syndicates to underwrite bond issues, and securities companies engaged in mere sales activities as sub-underwriters. At present, however, a bank cannot act as an underwriter, since article 65 of the Securities Exchange Law prohibits financial institutions from engaging in

---

41. 5 SHŌKEN KEIZAI KŌZA (Lectures on securities economics) 162 (SHIMURA AND NODA ED. 1968). The managing underwriter receives 23% and the other three, 19% respectively. FUJITA 101. This customary fixation of underwriting quota has been an obstacle to the development of an active debenture market. SŌGŌSEISAKU KENKYŪKAI, *Nippon no Kōsha-saishijō—Kin'yū Seijōka no Ikkan toshite* (Debt securities market in Japan—For the sake of financial normalization) 8 (TAKAHASHI AND FUKURA ED. 1966).

42. *See* p. 69 *infra.*

43. An explanation for this might involve a discussion of economics beyond the scope of this paper. In short, as has been suggested earlier (p. 2 *supra*), Japanese are generally said to be indirect-investment-minded, that is, they prefer savings deposits in banks to direct investment in business enterprises; and banks, especially in pre-war times, played dominant role in industries, somewhat similar to that of banks in Germany. After World War II inflation discouraged the public from investing in long-term debts.

44. The total amount of business corporation debentures (*jigyōsai*) issued in 1968 was 495 billion yen. Financial institutions (banks, trust companies, insurance companies and the like) purchased 73.6%, individuals 23.1%, investment trusts, 1.8%, and others 1.7%. 1969 MOF ANN. REP. Table 28 at 352–53.

45. FUJITA 99. The control was relaxed in 1956, but was revived soon after. 5 SHŌKEN KEIZAI KŌZA 52, 145, 159, 173 (SHIMURA AND NODA ED. 1968). *See also*, 1969 MOF ANN. REP. 14–16.

securities business.[46] This provision is derived from the American banking act,[47] but differs from the model in lack of restriction on acquisition of securities for an investment purpose. Therefore the goal of article 65 might lie in improving the business conditions of securities companies by enlarging their range of transactions rather than in protecting bank depositors, as sought by the U.S. act.[48] Indeed, thanks to this provision, securities companies secure a stable source of income by underwriting corporate debentures, in spite of the fact that the greater part of such debentures is still acquired by banks and other financial institutions as before. Securities companies are accused of appropriating "sleeping commissions" obtained without incurring any risk and without expending actual effort in underwriting.[49]

At present, in short, the securities market fails to perform its function with regard to corporate debentures, and improvement of the situation is crucial from the viewpoint of the national economy. Several organizations, both private and official and including the Securities Counseling Commission, are studying the problem of how to develop the market for corporate debentures by means and for the purpose of widespread absorption of corporate debentures by individuals and establishing fair market prices thereof.[50]

---

46. SEL, art. 65: "(1) Banks, trust companies and other financial institutions designated by a cabinet rule shall not engage for profit in the business enumerated in each item of paragraph 8 of article 2: *Provided* that a bank may engage in sales of a security on behalf of its customers to execute their written orders, or a bank, trust company or other financial institution designated by the cabinet rule may engage in sales of a security for the purpose of investment pursuant to other statutes or on behalf of cestui que trust pursuant to the trust agreement.

(2) The provision of the preceding paragraph shall not apply to a national government bond or to a local government bond, nor to any corporate or other debentures guaranteed by the government as to its redemption and payment of interest."

47. BANKING ACT OF 1933, sec. 24 (7), 12 U.S.C.A. § 24(7).

48. SUZUKI & KAWAMOTO 68–69.

49. Yasuhara (Managing Chief, National Association of Banks), *Genjō kara mite Ginkō no Shasai Hikiuke wa Datō ka* (Is underwriting of corporate debentures by a bank appropriate?), KIN'YŪ HŌMU JIJŌ (No. 62) 9 (1955); FUJITA 100.

50. SŌGŌSEISAKU KENKYŪKAI, *supra* note 41, at 8. Reports and recommendations of the Securities Counseling Commission are reprinted, *id.* at 187–200.

The size of the debt securities market has increased considerably in recent years. The following table shows the total amount of outstanding debt securities issued through public offering. 1968 MOF ANN. REP. 20.

Complexity of Statutes Along with this " democratization of corporate debentures " movement, the need for a comprehensive corporate debenture law must be taken into consideration in order to harmonize conflicting provisions in the Commercial Code, the Securities Exchange Law and the outworn Secured Debenture Trust Law. By way of example, how can the following labyrinth be resolved ? The Commercial Code presupposes that a company entrusted to solicit subscriptions for corporate debentures carries out the issuing procedure for the issuer[51] and provides that such entrusted company shall have all powers necessary to secure redemption of debentures on behalf of the debenture holders.[52] The Secured Debenture Trust Law provides that in the administration of a security for debentures, an entrusted company shall have all powers with regard to redemption and interest payment of debentures when entrusted by the issuer to solicit subscriptions therefor,[53] and that the same power shall be conferred upon a person, such entrusted company or otherwise, who has subscribed the total amount of the issue when such person distributes the debentures.[54] These provisions are based on the premise that the underwriting and the subsequent administration of corporate debentures are carried out by the same company or companies. Whereas the Securities Exchange Law prohibits a securities company from acting as an entrusted

---

End of year	Public bonds	Corporate debentures	Financial notes	Total
1955	71.9	229.8	374.1	675.8
1960	344.4	878.7	1,111.4	2,334.4
1966	1,328.0	1,674.7	3,019.9	6,022.6
1967	3,373.2	2,063.5	4,190.5	9,627.2

(1) The amount is shown in billion yen.

(2) Public bonds include national government bonds, local government bonds and bonds guaranteed by the government.

(3) As to financial notes, *see* p. 21 *supra.*

(4) In addition to this, at the end of 1967, the estimated amount of bonds issued by way of private placement reached 2,242.3 billion yen, excluding an unknown amount of local government bonds.

51. Comm. Code, art. 304.
52. Comm. Code, art. 309.
53. Secured Debenture Trust Law, art. 23.
54. Secured Debenture Trust Law, arts. 28 and 30.

company for corporate debentures on one hand,[55] and prohibits a financial institution from engaging in underwriting on the other hand,[56] purporting to allocate underwriting to securities companies and administration to financial institutions. What a contradiction! New legislation is the only solution to this problem.[57]

55. SEL, art. 45 para. 1. The Law Enacting the Amendments to the Commercial Code, art. 56 para. 1 (Law No. 73, 1938) provides that only banks and trust companies may be entrusted to distribute corporate debentures.

56. SEL, art. 65 para. 1. See *supra* note 46.

57. Scholars have made painstaking efforts to come up with interpretations minimizing contradictions in these provisions, products of patchy legislation. *See*, Ōtori, *Shasaihō* (Law of corporate debentures) 75, 111–24 (1958); 2 Nishihara, *Shōjihō Kenkyū* (Studies on commercial law) 221–233 (1963); Suzuki & Kawamoto 77–78.

CHAPTER 6

Registration of Securities

1. The Pre-Effective Period

No Distinction Between Pre- and Post-Filing Periods A public offering (*boshū*) or secondary distribution (*uridashi*) of securities is illegal and the security cannot be sold unless a registration statement is in effect.[1] This general prohibition corresponds to that of section 5 of the U.S. 1933 Act; but while the American act distinguishes between the pre-filing and the waiting periods and makes it possible by the use of a preliminary prospectus to offer the security and to solicit offers for its purchase during the waiting period,[2] Japanese law prohibits every offering or solicitation in connection with a public offering or secondary distribution both before and after the filing of a registration statement.[3]

The administrative authority has often cautioned banks not to receive payments of newly issued stocks for the issuers prior to effective registration.[4] To make subscribers pay for unregistered stock is an obvious violation, but not a few violative cases due to the parties' ignorance were seen just after the promulgation of the law.

Oral Solicitations As a result of unitary legislation, statutory prohibitions are not confined to interstate commerce or the mails, but extend to every

---

1. SEL, art. 4 para. 1, art. 15 para. 1. For definitions of " public offering " (*boshū*) and of " secondary distribution " (*uridashi*), *see* pp. 23–24 *supra.*

2. SECURITIES ACT OF 1933, sec. 5 (b) and (c), 15 U.S.C.A. § 77e (b), (c), as amended in 1954. *See also* Regulation C, Rule 433.

3. Regarding the extreme inconvenience deriving from this lack of distinction and proposals for amendments thereto, *see* pp. 53–54 *infra.*

4. Securities Exchange Commission Release (*shōshin*) No. 882, Nov. 18, 1948; Release (*shōshin*) No. 36, Feb. 8, 1949; Release (*shōshin*) No. 198, April 4, 1949.

Payments for stock must be made with specified banks or trust companies which are required to keep the fund on behalf of the issuer. COMM. CODE, art. 177 para. 2, arts. 178, 280–14 para. 1.

kind of offering or solicitation in connection with a public offering or secondary distribution, including oral offerings and advertisements.[5]

Underwriter's Preliminary Negotiation Unlike American law, which permits preliminary negotiations between an issuer and any underwriter or among underwriters,[6] Japanese law contains no such provision. Although such preliminary negotiations or agreements would seem to be illegal without an express provision, the better construction might permit them in the light of the purpose of the registration system which purports to protect investors and relates only to public offerings and secondary distributions to the public.[7]

Gray Area Several preparatory activities are regarded with suspicion as possibly violative of the law. Some issuers hold informal meetings with principal shareholders to explain reasons for the need to increase the company's capital. Resolutions by the boards of directors to issue additional shares are sometimes advertised in securities periodicals. Some managements disclose detailed information at press conferences about intended public offerings. Thus, statements amounting in effect to offerings with inaccurate information may be made before any step for registration is taken.

2. Registration Statement

Registrant The duty to register rests with the issuer of the securities, whether in the form of a public offering or a secondary distribution.[8] In the latter case, i.e., where a shareholder disposes his block of shares through the market, the registrant is not the shareholder, but the issuer. The shareholder can merely request the issuer to file a registration statement

---

5. Securities Exchange Commission Release (*shōshin*) No. 10, June 30, 1948.

6. SECURITIES ACT OF 1933, sec. 2 (3), 15 U.S.C.A. § 77b (3).

7. Sales between securities companies are exempt from the prospectus requirement. SEL, art. 15 para. 2. This exemption, however, unlike those of paragraphs 1 and 3 of the same article, does not extend to registration.

One of the draftsmen of the SEL, referring to exemptions provided by article 15 paragraph 3, which corresponds to section 4 of the U.S. 1933 Act, explains that the registration requirement is limited to securities transactions involving adhesive contract, and that the requirement does not extend to transactions wherein the prospective acquirer behaves of his own free will. YAMASHITA, *Kaisei Shōkentorihikihō Kaisetsu* (Explanation of amended securities exchange law) 29 (1948).

8. SEL, art. 4 para. 1.

with the Finance Minister. Where the shareholder controls the issuer, there may be no problem. As has been mentioned earlier,[9] however, the " control " concept has disappeared from the Japanese Securities Exchange Law. In the event that the issuer declines to prepare and file the registration statement, the shareholder must give up the secondary distribution.[10]

Form and Attached Documents The registrant must file with the Finance Minister three copies of registration statement using Form II.[11] The registration statement must be accompanied by the following documents: (a) the charter; (b) the prospectus; (c) a certificate showing unanimous consent by the incorporators relating to the issuance of securities, or a copy of the minutes of the shareholders' or the board of directors' meeting which approved the issuance; (d) a certificate of permission by an administrative authority if such is needed for increasing the amount of capital; (e) a copy of the underwriting agreement or of the trust deed; (f) a copy of the contract, if any, for leasing the business or the like; (g) a copy of the merger agreement or transfer of assets agreement, if referred to in the registration statement.[12]

3. Administrative Review

The Ministry of Finance reviews the registration statement and accompanying documents and, if any defects are found, can order the registrant, after opportunity for hearing, to file an amendment.[13]

---

9. *See* p. 31 *supra*.

10. In order to liquidate his shares, he is obliged to find one or several block purchaser(s) or to sell them piecemeal over a long period.

Where a secondary distribution is made without registration, the violators subject to civil and penal liabilities (SEL, arts. 16 and 198) may vary, depending upon the interpretation of the term " one who makes a secondary distribution." *See* pp. 31–32 *supra*.

11. SEL, art. 5 para. 1; Registration Rule, art. 9. Information required in a registration statement will be discussed in the next chapter in connection with a prospectus.

12. SEL, art. 5 para. 2; Registration Rule, art. 10. As to item (c), some explanation may be necessary. At the time of formation of a stock corporation, the incorporators (*hokkinin*) must decide by unanimous consent upon the following items, unless such matters are stipulated in the charter: (i) types and number of shares; (ii) issuing price of the shares; (iii) the amount of paid-in surplus where no-par-value shares are issued. COMM. CODE, art. 168–2. During the lifetime of a corporation, the board of directors determine the issuance of additional stock within the limit of authorized capital, unless the charter grants such power to the shareholder meeting. COMM. CODE, art. 280–2 para. 1.

13. SEL, art. 9, art. 10 para. 1.

Preliminary Review——Paternalism After the enactment of the Securities Exchange Law, it was customary for a registrant to submit a draft of the registration statement to the Finance Ministry. The authority reviewed the draft and instructed the registrant to correct the defects, if any, before the filing of a formal registration statement. Since the registration system had been unfamiliar to Japanese issuers, this practice of draft review played an educational role.

The Ministry took the position that, even after filing of a formal registration statement, an amendment order should be issued only where no alternative is available, and suggested that the registrant file a voluntary amendment pursuant to article 7 of the Securities Exchange Law.[14] The Ministry regarded the following circumstances as necessitating the filing of an amendment: (a) where it finds inappropriate descriptions or defects in form; (b) where the registrant indicates a plan to build or dispose of substantial facilities; (c) where the registrant's plants suffer damages from natural disasters or the like; (d) where the registrant is bound to dispose of the unsubscribed shares above the par value; (e) where the registrant decreases the number of additional shares as a result of an unsuccessful public offering; or (f) where the registrant plans to alter the subscription period or the date of payment for shares.[15]

Abolition of Preliminary Review In August 1965 the Finance Ministry discontinued the practice of advance review of registration statement drafts. One of the motives for such a decision was the recognition that such paternalistic treatment on the part of the supervisory authority had spoiled both issuers and accountants. Both had grown accustomed to depending on the Ministry's advice. An even worse tendency had developed, i.e., a false statement, if discovered, would not hurt the registrant since the informal advice, unlike the amendment order, lacked publicity. This abnormality culminated in business failures of well-known enterprises in 1964, revealing previous window-dressing in financial statements over a long period.[16]

This window-dressing concerned periodic reports. But the root of the

---

14. Ministry of Finance Release (*zōri*) No. 17594, Nov. 11, 1954.

15. Release *ibid.* It is doubtful that this release, which was issued at the time when advance review was practiced, is still valid, since the system has now disappeared. This release, however, remains extant in the *Shōken Roppō* (Compilation of laws, orders, releases and self-regulatory rules concerning securities).

16. *See* pp. 57–58 *infra.*

problem lay in the spoiled mentality of issuers and accountants, and registration statements were no exception. The Finance Ministry gradually realized that advance review of drafts was detrimental. In addition to abolishing the system, it also tightened supervision over issuers and accountants.[17]

4. Effective Date for Registration

Rule and Acceleration As a rule the registration statement becomes effective on the thirtieth day after the filing thereof.[18] When a voluntary amendment to the registration statement is filed prior to the effective date, the registration statement shall be considered to have been filed when such amendment was filed.[19] If, again, the Finance Minister orders the registrant to file an amendment, he designates the effective date.[20]

The thirty-day period may be accelerated where the Finance Minister deems the nature of the securities to be registered as readily understood by the public on account of the statements in the filing documents.[21] Prior to August 1965 acceleration was almost the rule by virtue of the advance review of drafts.[22] At present such advance review is not made, and the Ministry of Finance takes the position that the waiting period should not be accelerated.[23]

---

17. Ministry of Finance Release (*zōshō*) No. 450, Feb. 29, 1968.

18. SEL, art. 8 para. 1.

19. SEL, art. 8 para. 2.

20. SEL, art. 9 para. 2, art. 10 para. 2, art. 11.

21. SEL, art. 8 para. 3; Release *supra* note 14. Acceleration is also available in the case of an amended registration statement. SEL, art. 8 para. 4, art 9 para. 3, art. 10 para. 2.

22. Between January 1 and April 30, 1965, 28 registration statements were filed with the main office of the Finance Ministry. The time periods were as follows:

Days from Filing to Effective Date	Number of Cases
5 or less	1
6–10	2
11–15	10
16–20	1
21–25	8
26–30	6
total	28

1966 MOF Ann. Rep. 66.

23. Ministry of Finance Release, *supra.* note 17.

Stop Order The Finance Minister may, after notice and opportunity for hearing, issue a stop order suspending the effectiveness of the registration statement if it appears to him at any time that the registration statement includes any untrue statement of fact or omits any material fact required to be stated therein or necessary to render the statements therein not misleading.[24] When such statement has been amended in accordance with the stop order and the Minister of Finance regards the amendment as appropriate, he shall discontinue the stop order.[25] These provisions are copied, almost verbatim, from those of the U. S. 1933 Act,[26] but due to preliminary review of drafts the stop order has seldom been issued.

24. SEL, art. 10 para. 1.
25. SEL, art. 10 para. 3.
26. Securities Act of 1933, sec. 8(d), 15 U.S.C.A. § 77h(d).

CHAPTER 7

Disclosure to Investors

1. Prospectus

Methods of Disclosure In order for a person to sell a security not only must a registration statement be in effect as to the security,[1] but also a prospectus must be furnished to the purchaser prior to or at the time of the sale.[2] Apart from this requirement as to a prospectus, the Commercial Code provides that a subscription for stock or debenture is to be made by the use of a subscription form, and it stipulates items to be stated therein.[3] The

1. SEL, art. 15 para. 1.
2. SEL, art. 15 para. 2.
3. COMM. CODE, arts. 175, 280–6, 280–14 and 301. The following are required items to be included in the stock subscription form used at the time of incorporation (those marked with an asterisk* are items required for the stock subscription form used after corporate formation): (a) date on which the charter was attested and name of the notary public who attested it; (b) mandatory statements in the charter, i.e., (i) purpose of the issuing corporation, (ii)* corporate name, (iii)* total number of authorized shares, (iv)* par value of a share of stock, (v) number of shares to be issued at the time of incorporation (* issued shares), and a statement as to whether they are of par value or no par value and the respective numbers, (vi) stated value of no-par-value shares, if any (* paid in surplus), (vii) location of the principal office, (viii) method of public notices, and (ix) names and addresses of incorporators; (c) provisions, if any, as to the period of existence or causes for dissolution of the corporation; (d)* particulars as to each class of shares and the number thereof; (e)* stipulation, if any, that transfer of stock is subject to approval by the board of directors; (f)* provisions, if any, as to the distribution of interest prior to the commencement of business; (g)* redemption provisions, if any; (h) stipulations concerning compensation to incorporators and contribution-in-kind (* particulars as to contribution-in-kind); (i) subscriptions by incorporators; (j)* banks or trust companies to receive stock payment; (k) statement that a share subscription may be rescinded in the event that the general organization meeting is not completed by a fixed date; (l)* names, addresses and offices of the transfer agent and/or registrar, if any. A stock subscription form may be replaced by a subscription warrant. *Cf.* p. 15 *supra.* Items to be stated in a subscription warrant, in addition to those marked with an asterisk above, are as follows: (i) statement that the certificate is a subscription warrant; (ii) particulars as to the stock covered by subscription right (class, par value or no par value, and number); (iii) statement that the subscription right expires upon failure to subscribe within the specified period. COMM. CODE, art. 280–6–2 para. 2.

A subscription for stock by incorporators (those who have signed the corporate charter) may be made in writing only, and does not require the use of a stock subscription form. COMM. CODE, art. 169.

Securities Exchange Law, however, added the prospectus requirement not only because the statements in a subscription form do not give sufficient information for investment, but also because the prescribed subscription form is not applicable to a secondary distribution of securities, regardless of their volume.[4]

Exemptions from the Prospectus Requirement Since the aim of the prospectus requirement is the protection of the investing public, the law itself provides for certain exceptions. A prospectus need not accompany the transaction in the following cases: (1) where a securities company sells the security to another securities company;[5] (2) where the transaction is made by any person other than by an issuer, one who makes a secondary distribution, underwriter or securities company; (3) where an issuer or one who makes a secondary distribution sells the security other than through a public offering or secondary distribution; (4) where the transaction is made by a securities company or by one who acted as underwriter with respect to the security involved after the expiration of one year from the effective date of the registration statement for such security, provided that transactions as to securities constituting the unsold allotment to such dealer as a participant in the public offering or secondary distribution are excluded; (5) where a securities company sells the security to customers upon the latters' orders so long as such orders are not obtained through the former's solicitation.[6]

More simply, unless a sale of securities constitutes a part of a public offering or secondary distribution, a statutory prospectus is not required.[7]

Where a statutory prospectus is not required, a prospectus may still be used. The content of such prospectus is not regulated, except that a prospectus used in connection with an offering exempted from registration because of small amount must state, on its cover or legibly on the first page, that the security is exempt from the registration requirement.[8]

Definition of a Prospectus The term "prospectus" is defined by the law as "any instrument given to the public, for the purpose of a public offering or secondary distribution, containing explanations as to the business of the

---

4. FUJITA 117.

5. SEL, art. 15 para. 2 proviso.

6. SEL, art. 15 para. 3. In these cases, i.e., (2) through (5) in the above text, transactions may be made without effective registration.

7. SEL, art. 15 para. 2 main clause.

8. SEL, art. 4 para. 2; Registration Rule, art. 7.

issuer of the security to be offered.[9] Whenever an instrument or advertisement refers to the business of the issuer, it is considered a prospectus regardless of its heading, and required to state the same information as contained in the registration statement.[10] On the other hand, unlike the American act,[11] the law does not refer to " radio or television," and the term "instrument" (*bunsho*) literally includes only writings. This problem will have to be solved in the future.

Preparation of a Prospectus In case of a public offering or secondary distribution, the issuer must prepare a prospectus.[12] The information required in a prospectus, as a rule, shall be the same as contained in the registration statement;[13] but on one hand, there may be omitted from a prospectus any information which the Finance Minister may designate by rules as unnecessary in the public interest or for the protection of investors, and on the other hand, additional information which the Minister may likewise designate as necessary should be stated in the prospectus.[14] The Ministerial Rule prescribes some additional items to be stated in a prospectus, whereas it does not enumerate items which can be omitted but merely provides that those items which can be omitted or summarized without harm to the public interest or to the protection of investors may be omitted or summarized.[15] Such items are enumerated in administrative releases.[16]

Information Required in a Prospectus Items to be stated in a prospectus according to Form II for registration statement are as follows (those which

---

9. SEL, art. 2 para. 10.

10. Securities Exchange Commission Release (*shōshin*) No. 10, June 30, 1948.

11. Securities Act of 1933, sec. 2(10), 15 U.S.C.A. § 77b(10).

12. SEL, art. 13 para. 1.

13. SEL, art. 13 para. 2.

14. SEL, art. 13 paras. 3 and 4. The items in a prospectus need not be stated in the same order as in the registration statement. Registration Rule, art. 11.

15. Registration Rule, art. 11.

16. Ministry of Finance Release (*zōri*) No. 20364, Sept. 10, 1953; Release (*zōri*) No. 9819, Sept. 28, 1956; Release (*zōri*) No. 6162, July 30, 1962.

Where one or more items are omitted and/or summarized, it is necessary to state, on the cover or legibly on the first page of the prospectus, which items are omitted and/or summarized, and to note that detailed contents of those items are available by inspection of the registration statement kept at the Department of Securities, Ministry of Finance, at such and such securities exchange, and at the principal and branch offices of the issuing corporation. Registration Rule, art. 12; Ministry of Finance Release (*zōri*) No. 6162, July 30, 1962.

may be summarized or partially omitted are marked with an asterisk*)[17]:

(1) Outlook of the registrant corporation—(a) date on which the registrant was incorporated, (b) purpose of the registrant, (c) amount of stated capital, (d) capital structure, (e)* description of shareholders, market prices of stock and dividends, (f)* directors and auditors,[18] (g)* description of employees;

(2) History of registrant and description of its operation and facilities;

(3)* Description of business;

(4) Financial situation—(a)* financial statements,[19] (b) principal assets, liabilities, income and expenses, (c) miscellaneous—circumstances occurring after the date of the balance sheet which materially affect or may affect the financial status;[20]

(5) Plan of public offering—(a) capital stock to be issued, (b) methods of offering, (c) incorporators and their subscriptions, (d)* underwriting agreements, (e) terms of the public offering, (f) debentures to be issued, (g)* underwriting and trust agreement for debentures;

(6) Use of proceeds by the registrant—(a)* amount of costs and proceeds of the issue, (b) intended use of proceeds;

(7) Rewards conferred to incorporators;[21]

(8) Contribution-in-kind;

(9) Contracted assets to be obtained after incorporation;

(10) Terms of secondary distribution or entrustment thereof;

(11) Miscellaneous—(1) statement of effective registration, (b) price of the security, (c) table of items omitted or summarized, if any.

---

17. SEL, art. 5 para. 1; Registration Rule, arts. 9 and 12, Form II thereunder; Releases *supra* note 16.

18. Information required as to this item includes position, name and address, birthdate, brief personal history, and shareholding (class, par value or no par value, number). Their remuneration need not be disclosed nor their personal interest in financial transactions. *Cf.* Items 17 and 20 of Form S-1 under the Securities Act of 1933. *See also* p. 56 *infra.*

19. Consolidated financial statements are not required. The Business Accounting Counseling Commission presented "An Opinion Concerning Consolidated Financial Statements" on May 11, 1967. The Commission stressed the need for introducing such statements and enumerated principles and standards for their consolidation. At the same time, however, the Commission pointed out that several obstacles, including provisions in the tax law, must be overcome before consolidation is statutorily required.

20. Pending legal proceedings are not specifically designated as an item to be stated, although this may be included by construction. *Cf.* Item 12 of Form S-1 under the Securities Act of 1933.

21. Stock option is not popular in Japan.

Other Remarks It is illegal to represent that the Minister of Finance has passed upon the accuracy or adequacy of the prospectus or that he has guaranteed the value of the security on the ground that the registration statement has become effective.[22] Unlike the provision in American law,[23] however, positive statement to that effect is not required.

When a prospectus is used more than one year after the effective date of the registration statement, the information contained therein must be valid for a date not more than six months prior to such use.[24]

Proposed Amendments as to Prospectus It is true that the introduction of the security registration and the prospectus regulation represented a great advance in Japanese securities regulation. But there still remains a problem derived from the direct import of the American model into a country with a different underwriting practice.

As noted earlier,[25] right offering is the prevailing method of issuing additional capital stock, and it is customary for Japanese corporations to issue stock to their existing shareholders at par value, even when the market price thereof is far above the par. Shareholders, therefore, rarely fail to subscribe for their proportional new stock.[26] Since they are forced, in a

22. SEL, art. 23.
23. *Cf.* Rule 425, 17 C.F.R. § 230.425.
24. SEL, art. 14 para. 1.
25. *See* p. 3 *supra.*
26. If there is no considerable difference between the market price and the par value, the issuer makes the offering attractive by transferring a certain amount from a revaluation reserve fund (*saihyōka tsumitatekin*) into the stated capital account, so that shareholders may be freed from payment of a part of the par value.

The Law Concerning Revaluation of Assets (*Shisan saihyōkahō*) (Law No. 110, 1950) has made it possible for individuals, partnerships and corporations to revalue their assets, in order to enable reasonable depreciation thereof during the period of post-war inflation. Where a corporation writes up its assets, it must retain the increased amount as the revaluation reserve fund (art. 102). The use of this fund is restricted to payment of revaluation tax, making up of a deficit, and transfer into stated capital or the like (art. 107).

The Law Concerning Transfer of Revaluation Reserve Fund into Stated Capital in Stock Corporations (*Kabushiki-gaisha no saihyōka tsumitatekin no shihonkumiire ni kansuru hōritsu*) (Law No. 146, 1951) prescribes the procedure for transfer of this reserve fund into stated capital. A stock corporation may (1) transfer the reserve into stated capital without issuing new shares; (2) transfer the reserve into stated capital, distributing new paid-up shares to the shareholders (in substance, a kind of stock dividend); or (3) use the reserve fund for partial payment for stock to be issued to the shareholders at par value. This last is actually a sort of discount issue of par-value stock. A vast amount of shares were issued in this manner. However, since almost all corporations with the exception of electric power companies have disposed of this reserve fund in various ways, issuance of shares by use of this fund is not as common as before. *See* TAKEUCHI, *Jōyokin no Shihonkumiire* (Transfer of reserve fund into stated capital) 28–32 (1962).

The latter statute concerning the transfer is due to expire on March 31, 1973.

sense, to subscribe in order not to lose their proportional interests, prospectuses play a diminished role in their investment decisions. True, shareholders have the alternative of selling their old stock "*cum*-right." But, again, due to the absolute prohibition of public offering prior to the effective date, shareholders cannot obtain prospectuses until after the record date, when the old stock sells only "*ex*-right."

For these reasons the National Association of Corporate Departments for Shareholder Administration[27] and the committee for commercial legislation of the Tokyo Chamber of Commerce made proposals in 1957 to a similar effect. In short, they proposed that registration statements and prospectuses should be simplified and review thereof by the authorities should be made more promptly, by means of a business report to shareholders,[28] in place of a prospectus, required to state the plan of public offering and a summary of material information given in the periodic report filed with the authorities.[29] Thus far no legislative step has been taken in this direction, nor has any amendment comparable to that of 1954 to the American 1933 act been made, although the latter is taken into consideration in the current reform project.

After the publication of the "Wheat Report,"[30] discussions reopened in Japan to the effect that emphasis should be shifted to continuous disclosures from registration statements.

---

27. In several districts of Japan corporate employees in charge of shareholder administration organize groups to meet and study common problems, legal and otherwise, such as *Tokyo Kabushiki Konwakai* which publishes the monthly periodical "*Kaihō*" (Report) or *Osaka Kabushiki Kondankai* which issues the monthly "*Kiroku*" (Report). These local organizations form a national association, which corresponds to the American Society of Corporate Secretaries, Inc. (*Kabushiki* are shares of stock and *konwakai* or *kondankai* means conference.)

28. A business report (*eigyō hōkokusho*) is one of the corporate reports (*keisanshorui*) subject to shareholders' approval. COMM. CODE, art. 281 item 3. But there is no regulation governing the content of a business report, whereas balance sheets and income statements are regulated by the Commercial Code, the Corporate Reports Regulation and the Financial Statement Regulation. A business report usually announces recent company activities and achievements and contains an address by the president stressing optimistic prospects for the future.

29. *Cf.* Yazawa, *Mokuromisho-seido no Kaisei Mondai* (Problems of improving the prospectus system), SHŌJI HŌMU KENKYŪ (No. 81) 2 (1957); FUJITA, 131.

30. DISCLOSURE TO INVESTORS: A REAPPRAISAL OF FEDERAL ADMINISTRATIVE POLICIES UNDER THE '33 AND' 34 ACTS (1969).

2. Periodic Report

Duty to File Issuing corporations with outstanding securities, for which a registration has become effective, are required to file a periodic report (*yūkashōken hōkokusho*) with the Finance Minister within three months after the expiration of each accounting period.[31] Form III to be used for a periodic report enumerates approximately the same items as those in Form II for a registration statement.[32]

Thus the duty to file a periodic report is linked with the registration system. Those corporations whose securities have not been sold by means of a public offering or secondary distribution are not subject to supervision by the Finance Minister, no matter how active trading may be in the over-the-counter market. On the other hand, once a registration statement has been filed, the issuing corporation must continue to file periodic reports until its dissolution, irrespective of diminishing size and number of shareholders and decreasing involvement in securities transactions.

With a view toward eliminating this incongruity, an amendment to the Securities Exchange Law is under consideration. It is possible that a disclosure system for the trading market may be established, apart from the registration system, along the lines of the 1964 amendment to the U. S. 1934 Act and the Wheat Report.[33]

---

31. SEL, art. 24 para. 1.

A periodic report corresponds to an annual report under the U.S. act. The term "periodic report" is chosen instead of "annual report" because most Japanese corporations have semi-annual accounting periods. The statute requires only that a corporation shall hold a regular meeting of shareholders once a year, or, where the corporation pays dividends twice or more often a year, it shall hold the meeting for each accounting period. COMM. CODE, art. 234. Payment of interim dividends is prohibited. *Cf.* COMM. CODE, art. 281 item 5, art. 283, art. 290 para. 1. It has been customary that corporations pay dividends semi-annually. Recently, however, the number of corporations with annual instead of semi-annual accounting periods has been increasing. The proposed bill amending the Commercial Code provides that a corporation may pay interim dividends, within a certain limit of distributable surplus, by a resolution of the board of directors. Securities exchanges ask listed corporations having an annual accounting period to file an interim report (*chūkan hōkokusho*) with the exchange, on the basis of a general provision in the listing agreement to the effect that a listed corporation shall surrender statements required by the exchange.

32. Registration Rule, arts. 14 and 15, Form III thereunder.

33. Sakano, *Shōkentorihikihō no Mondaiten to sono Haikei* (Problems in the Securities Exchange Law and their backgrounds) SHŌJI HŌMU KENKYŪ (No. 487) 5–6 (1969).

Administrative Review The Finance Minister has the same power with respect to periodic reports as in the case of registration statements——to issue amendment orders and stop orders.[34] Administrative review tended to be perfunctory and culminated in failures of well-known corporations in 1964, revealing accumulated window-dressings. The Ministry of Finance adopted a strong stand vis-à-vis issuing corporations as well as accountants. Along with the discontinuation of advance review of registration statement drafts,[35] the authority strengthened its power to review periodic reports, affirming its readiness to impose statutory sanctions against false statements in the reports.[36]

Periodic Reports on Listed Securities Issuing corporations whose securities are listed on a securities exchange, except those which file periodic reports with the Finance Minister, are required to submit periodic reports on listed securities (*jōjōyūkashōken hōkokusho*) to the securities exchange.[37] The form to be used is Form III, the same as that required for the periodic report mentioned above.[38] The provision concerning voluntary amendment to a registration statement is applicable here,[39] but no one has the power to issue an amendment or stop order with regard to this type of periodic report.

3. CPA Audit

Auditors and Accountants Every stock corporation must maintain one or more auditors (*kansayaku*) elected by shareholder meeting, and corporate reports must be audited by such auditors prior to their submission to the

---

34. SEL, art. 24 para. 2.
35. *See* p. 46 *supra*.
36. Ministry of Finance Release (*zōshō*) No. 450, Feb. 29, 1968.

Between September 1965 and December 1967, 2,349 corporations filed periodic reports with the Finance Ministry, which investigated 120 dubious cases and found 53 cases of window-dressing. Fourteen corporations submitted voluntary amendments. The authority issued two amendment orders and prosecuted two corporations. Disciplinary action was taken against 22 accountants. During the 1968 calender year the situation improved slightly. 1969 MOF Ann. Rep. Table 26 at 54.

37. SEL, art. 118 para. 1.
38. Exchange Rule, art. 8.
39. SEL, art. 118 para. 2.

regular meeting of shareholders.[40] Auditing of this sort, however, is not sufficient for the protection of investors mainly because of the auditors' actual dependence to the management. Consequently the Securities Exchange Law, after the model of U. S. Rule 2–01 of Regulation S-X, requires that financial statements be certified by an independent certified public accountant, but such provision applies only to statements of listed corporations and corporations issuing securities registered or to be registered.[41]

Accountants are regulated by the Certified Public Accountant Law,[42] and their auditing procedure is governed by a ministerial rule.[43]

Exemptions Banks, trust companies, insurance companies and certain other corporations are exempt from the requirement of CPA audit certification.[44] This exemption, it is argued, is based upon the fact that these enterprises are subject to strict regulation by the government. Although they are exempted only " for the time being," it is unlikely that they will be deprived of this vested privilege in the foreseeable future.

The San'yō Steel Case Until recently many of the audit reports by public accountants simply stated " adequate " with respect to the financial statements they had audited, and the reports were regarded with less importance than anticipated at the time of the passage of the law. In 1964 and

---

40. COMM. CODE, art. 170 para. 1, arts. 183, 273 through 280 and 281, art. 282 para. 1. The term " corporate reports " (*keisanshorui*) refers to documents enumerated in article 281 of the Commercial Code: (i) inventory sheet, (ii) balance sheet, (iii) income statement, (iv) business report, and (v) surplus appropriation plan. These documents, except the inventory sheet, must be approved by the regular meeting of shareholders. COMM. CODE, art. 283 para. 1. As to why the term " regular meeting " is used instead of annual meeting, *see* note 31 *supra*. With regard to a " business report," *see* note 28 *supra*.

41. SEL, art. 193–2 para. 1 ; SEL Enforcement Rule, art. 8. The term " financial statements " (*zaimushohyō*), as opposed to " corporate reports " in the preceding note, refers to accounting documents required to be filed as a part of a registration statement, periodic report or periodic report on listed securities under the Securities Exchange Law: (i) balance sheet, (ii) income statement, (iii) surplus statement, (iv) surplus appropriation statement or deficit reconciliation statement, and (v) schedules. SEL, art. 193 ; Financial Statement Regulation, art. 1 para. 1.

Securities exchanges require that financial statements included in an interim report (note 31 *supra*) be certified by a CPA.

42. *Kōninkaikeishihō* (Law No. 103, 1948).

43. *Zaimushohyō no Kansashōmei ni kansuru Shōrei* (Ministerial rule concerning audit certification for financial statements) (Ministry of Finance Rule No. 12, 1957).

44. SEL Enforcement Rule, Supplementary Provision § 6.

the first quarter of 1965, however, not a few big enterprises encountered financial deadlock, culminating in the catastrophe of San'yō Steel Company, and the public began to pay much more attention to audit reports, as many cases were revealed where financial statements turned out to be false.

The San'yō Steel Co. case is indeed comparable with the famous case involving McKesson and Robbins, Inc.,[45] in the magnitude of the fraud, the manner in which it was accomplished, and the sensational developments following the exposure. On March 3, 1965, San'yō Steel Co., a listed corporation with capital stock of 7.4 billion yen and 3,700 employees, suddenly applied for corporate reorganization on the ground of insolvency, after continuous distribution of 10 to 12 percent dividends. Investigation by the authority revealed that the company had accounted fictitious earnings since 1959 amounting in total to about 7 billion yen, that the management had received more than three times as much remuneration as indicated in financial statements, and that the certified public accountant had knowingly reported these fictitious statements as adequate.[46]

Apart from criminal and civil proceedings against the company and its president, the Ministry of Finance suspended the registration of the certified public accountant.[47] Many similar cases of window-dressing accounting have occurred.[48]

Its Aftermath: Tightening Control The Ministry tightened the standards for reviewing registration statements and periodic reports, and declared that it would exercise stricter control over accountants.[49] In order to

45. In the Matter of McKesson & Robbins, Inc., Report on Investigation (1940); RAPPAPORT, SEC ACCOUNTING PRACTICE AND PROCEDURE 4·3–4·11 (2d ed., rev. print. 1966).

46. Kawamoto and Kanzaki, " *San'yōkō* " *Kaishakōsei-jiken no Hōteki Kentō* (Legal study on the corporate reorganization case of San'yō Steel Co.), SHŌJI HŌMU KENKYŪ (No. 355) 2 et seq. (1965); Harada (Reorganization trustee for the San'yō Tokushuseikō K.K.) v. Ogino *et al.*, HANREI JIHŌ (No. 445) 19 (Kobe Dist. Ct., Himeji Branch, Apr. 11, 1966).

47. SHŌJI HŌMU KENKYŪ (No. 358) 22 (1965).

48. Kodama (Reorganization trustee for Sun Wave Kōgyō K.K.) v. Shibasaki, HANREI JIHŌ (No. 470) 56 (Tokyo Dist. Ct., Dec. 23, 1966); 1966 MOF ANN. REP. 63–67; 1967 MOF ANN. REP. 43–48; 1968 MOF ANN. REP. 77–79; 1969 MOF ANN. REP. 55–56; NIPPON KEIZAI SHINBUN SHŌKENBU (ED.), *Funshoku Kessan* (Window-dressing accounting) (1966).

49. Message, Sep. 30, 1965, SHŌJI HŌMU KENKYŪ (No. 360) 63 (1965); Ministry of Finance Release (*zōshō*) No. 1654, May 30, 1966.

improve the quality and maintain the independence of accountants, a number of amendments to the Certified Public Accountant Law were made, including establishment of a national association of certified public accountants with compulsory membership and the organization of accounting corporations.[50] The Ministry of Finance declared that it would publish monthly a list of audit reports containing an adverse opinion or a disclaimer of opinion.[51] Securities exchanges, at least those of Tokyo and Osaka, now publish in their periodicals all audit reports of their listed corporations.[52]

Proposed Amendments to the Commercial Code Under the present law financial statements have to be audited by a CPA. Financial statements are filed with the Ministry of Finance within three months after the close of each accounting period. The CPA's audit is made after the shareholders' meeting has approved the corporate reports, for which a corporate auditor's opinion suffices. Financial statements must be prepared in accordance with the Financial Statements Regulation, whereas a part of the corporate reports are regulated by the Corporate Reports Regulation administered by the Ministry of Justice. Balance sheets and income statements are subject to both of these regulations.

Efforts have been made to achieve harmony between these two regulations as well as to secure better protection of investors. Differences between the two regulations are being reduced to a minimum by virtue of amendments to both of them. The Legislative Council, in November 1966, immediately after consummation of its work amending the Commercial Code, began an investigation into the auditor system. The Council completed the final plan of amendment on March 30, 1970.

The plan contains a provision that stock corporations with 100 million yen or more stated capital shall have their corporate reports audited by a

---

50. Law No. 85, 1966. An accounting corporation (*kansahōjin*) is a special type of corporation consisting of five or more CPAs. Many provisions of the Commercial Code concerning a partnership corporation (*gōmei-gaisha*) are applicable *mutatis mutandis* to accounting corporations. Certified Public Accountant Law, arts. 34–2 through 34–22. As of the end of March 1969, 14 accounting corporations were in operation. 1969 MOF ANN. REP. Table 28 at 58.

51. Message, *supra* note 49. *See also* note 36 *supra*.

52. SHŌKEN of Tokyo Securities Exchange and IMBESUTOMENTO of Osaka Securities Exchange, both of which are published monthly.

certified public accountant.[53] This means that in these corporations balance sheet, income statement and other documents must be audited by a professional accountant before their submission to the shareholders' meeting. The plan extends the power of an auditor (*kansayaku*) by granting him the power to supervise directors.[54] A general provision is to be included to the effect that fair and just accounting practices shall be taken into consideration in intepretation of accounting provisions.[55]

4. Proxy Regulation

In General The proxy system is utilized to a great extent both by listed and unlisted corporations.[56] Several fierce proxy contests have been waged for corporate control.[57] The practice of tender offer (take-over bid) has not yet arisen in Japan. Unlike proxy solicitation, tender offers are not regulated by any special statutory provisions.

Coverage of the Regulation Article 194 of the Securities Exchange Law provides that any person shall not solicit proxies with regard to shares issued by a listed corporation in contravention to the cabinet rule. Therefore, only listed corporations are subject to the Proxy Regulation. The Regulation itself provides three exemptions: (a) where a person other than the issuing corporation or its management solicits proxies from less than ten

---

53. *Shōhō no Ichibu o Kaiseisuru Hōritsuan-yōkō* (Gist of a bill amending a part of the Commercial Code), Item 14(1). Banks and other companies exempted from the audit requirement under the SEL will also be exempt for a certain transitional period from the coming CPA audit requirement under the Commercial Code.

54. *Id.* Item 1. This represents, in a sense, a revival of the pre-1950 statute.

55. *Id.* Item 15 (1) ii. In practice, " fair and just accounting practices " refer to the Business Accounting Principles (*Kigyōkaikei gensoku*), upon which the Financial Statements Regulation is based. The " Principles " and the regulation were revised so that the gap between them and the Corporate Reports Regulation might be minimized. As to interim dividend of Item 13 of the plan, *see* note 31 *supra*.

56. A 1967 survey revealed that about half of the listed corporations and more than half of the unlisted corporations solicit proxies, even in cases where the shareholder meeting makes only ordinary resolutions for which the quorum requirement may be dispensed with. Shōji Hōmu Kenkyū (No. 427) 16 (1967). It follows that where a special resolution is required, for which a quorum is indispensable, almost all of the publicly held corporations solicit proxies.

57. Yazawa and Mitooka, *Shihaiken no Sōdatsu to Kabunushisōkai* (Struggles for control and shareholder meetings), 17 Shihō 41 (1957).

shareholders; (2) where a solicitation is made by the use of a tombstone ad; and (3) where a beneficiary owner solicits a proxy from the nominee.[58]

Proxy Materials The proxy form to be used for solicitation must provide a means whereby the person solicited can specify a choice between approval or disapproval of each matter referred to therein.[59] It is customary that the name(s) of the agent(s) is not printed on the proxy form.

One who solicits proxies shall furnish the person solicited with a proxy statement, prior to or simultaneous with the solicitation.[60] Items of information to be presented in a proxy statement are enumerated in the regulation.[61] False statements and material omissions are prohibited.[62]

A copy of the proxy form and proxy statement must be filed with the Ministry of Finance simultaneously with the mailing of them to the shareholders.[63] This means that there is no administrative review before the dissemination of proxy materials.[64]

Violative Solicitation and Voting One who has violated provisions of the Proxy Regulation is subject to penal sanction.[65] The Finance Minister has the power to make application before the court to issue a cease and desist order against the violator.[66] Neither of these sanctions has been invoked thus far.

Majority scholarly opinion holds that the validity of a shareholder meeting resolution is not affected by incompliance with the Proxy Regulation nor by the fact that the agent has failed to abide by the voting instructions

58. Proxy Regulation, art. 9.

59. Proxy Regulation, art. 3. The Commercial Code requires that a proxy be in writing and that such be given for each single shareholder meeting only. COMM. CODE, art. 239 paras. 3 and 4.

60. Proxy Regulation, art. 1.

61. Proxy Regulation, art. 2. Information required is less extensive and less detailed than that required by the U.S. Schedule 14 A, 17 C.F.R. § 240.14a–101.

62. Proxy Regulation, art. 7.

63. Proxy Regulation, art. 6. The term "simultaneously" is construed to mean "within the same day at the latest." Securities Exchange Commission Release (*shōsō*) No. 173, June 15, 1950.

64. The original Proxy Regulation required that a draft of proxy materials be filed with the Ministry ten days prior to the mailing of those materials to the shareholders (art. 6). This advance review system was abolished by the 1955 amendment to the Regulation, mainly due to pressure by business interests.

65. SEL, art. 205 item 1.

66. SEL, art. 187.

written on the proxy forms.[67] The contrary view seems to be more persuasive.[68]

5. Access to Detailed Information

Public Inspection The Ministry of Finance keeps registration statements, periodic reports and their amendments on file for five years, and the public can inspect these documents at its office.[69] The issuer of securities has to keep the copies of its registration statement, periodic report and amendments thereof at its principal office and at those offices located in prefectures where more than five percent of its shareholders reside, and has to allow the public to inspect these copies.[70] Furthermore, listed corporations are required to file with the securities exchange a copy of the registration statement and a copy of the periodic report without delay after its effective date, and the public can inspect them at such a securities exchange.[71] Periodic reports on listed securities must be likewise retained for public inspection.[72]

Where the issuer wishes to withhold certain information relating to business secrets from public inspection, the issuer can so apply to the

---

67. 1 Ōsumi, *Zentei Kaishahōron* (Treatise on corporation law) 33 (rev. ed. 1959); 1 S. Tanaka, *Kaishahō Shōron* (Details on corporation law) 390 (1967); 1 Ishii, *Kaishahō* (Corporation law) 247 (1967); Ōmori, *Giketsuken* (Voting right), in 3 Kabushiki-gaishahō Kōza, 934 (Tanaka ed. 1956); Sakai, *Kabunushisōkai ni okeru Giketsuken no Dairikōshi no Kan'yū ni tsuite* (On the solicitation of proxies for shareholder meetings), 7 Shōdai Ronshū 74–77 (Kobe College of Commerce, 1951). Their argument is that a resolution by shareholder meeting is rescindable only where the procedure of convening the meeting or the method of resolution has been illegal or grossly unfair. Comm. Code, art. 247 para. 1. Solicitation of proxies does not comprise " the procedure of convening the meeting," because a corporation is not obligated to solicit them. Besides, it is a general principle that where an agent fails to comply with the principal's instruction, the agent's conduct is nonetheless valid vis-à-vis third parties, although the agent is liable to the principal.

68. Yazawa, *Giketsuken no Dairikōshi* (Voting by proxy), Kaihō (No. 119) 36 (Tokyo Kabushiki Konwakai, 1961); Hishida, *Kabunushi no Giketsukenkōshi to Kaishashihai* (Voting by shareholders and corporate control) 108, 120 (1960); Tatsuta, *Kabushikigaisha no Ininjōseido* (Proxy system in stock corporation), 21 Imbesutomento 36 (Osaka Securities Exchange, 1968); Sakaino v. Ōmi Kenshi Bōseki K.K., 20 Kōsai minshū 411 (Osaka High Ct., Sep. 26, 1967). *Cf.* J.I. Case Co. v. Borak, 377 U.S. 426 (1964).

69. SEL, art. 25 para. 1; Registration Rule. art. 17.

70. SEL, art. 25 para. 2; Registration Rule, arts. 18 and 19.

71. SEL, arts. 6, 12, 24, 25 para. 3; Registration Rule, art. 20.

72. SEL, art. 118 para. 2; Exchange Rule, art. 9.

Finance Minister for his approval. Upon approval such information is not available to public inspectors and the issuer may delete such items from the copies to be filed with securities exchanges.[73]

Right of Inspection under the Commercial Code Aside from these opportunities for public access to information, the Commercial Code also contains provisions on disclosure. A corporation is required to keep at its principal office the inventory sheet, balance sheet, business report, income statement, surplus appropriation plan and auditor's report for one week before the date of each regular meeting.[74] Any shareholder or creditor of the corporation may, at any time during business hours, inspect these documents and may request a copy or an excerpt of such documents, paying such fees as are fixed by the corporation.[75] A corporation shall give public notice of the balance sheet without delay after its approval by the regular meeting of shareholders.[76]

A corporation must prepare schedules of the corporate reports within four months after the end of each accounting period and keep them at its principal and branch offices. Any shareholder may, at any time during business hours, inspect or make extracts from the schedules, and may request a copy or an excerpt of the schedules, paying such fees as are fixed by the corporation.[77]

Any shareholder or shareholders having not less than one-tenth of the outstanding shares also may inspect or make extracts from the books, records and documents of the account, subject to the corporation's right to reject it in limited cases.[78]

---

73. SEL, art. 25 paras. 4 and 5.
74. COMM. CODE, art. 282 para. 1.
75. COMM. CODE, art. 282 para. 2.
76. COMM. CODE, art. 283 para. 2.
77. COMM. CODE, art. 293–5.
78. COMM. CODE, arts. 293–6 and 293–7.

Chapter 8

Mergers, Reorganizations and Conversions

1. Mergers and No-Sale Rule

Mergers Exempt: A Different Approach Unlike American law, Japanese law contains no definition of the term " sale,"[1] nor a rule exempting certain corporate actions for which the vote of a majority of stockholders is required and binding.[2] What is subject to the registration requirement is not a " sale " itself but a public offering or a secondary distribution, in other words, an offer of securities as against unspecified many persons with a uniform term.[3] Therefore the question at stake is whether or not a transaction falls within the category of a public offering or secondary distribution.

In the case of a statutory merger or consolidation, giving stockholders of merged or dissolving corporations shares of the merging or consolidated corporation is not construed as a public offering. One of the reasons for such exemption lies in the gratuitous nature of the transaction.[4] What is meant by gratuity here is that shareholders are not requested to contribute additional money, their only obligation being to surrender their present share certificates, although this is nothing but a " consideration " in the American view. Another reason might be found in the fact, like the no-sale theory, that the shareholders have no alternative but to accept the allotment, i.e., the element of " solicitation " indispensable for a public

---

1. Securities Act of 1933, sec. 2(3), 15 U.S.C.A. § 77 b(3).

2. Rule 133, 17 C.F.R. § 230.133.

3. *See* p. 22 *supra*.

4. Securities Exchange Commission Release (*shōhatsu*) No. 73, June 24, 1949. Shareholders have no choice but to subscribe. Suzuki and others, *Kabushikigaisha no Gappei* (Mergers by stock corporations) 145–46 (rev. ed. 1963).

A fortiori, registration is not necessary for securities issued to the existing shareholders in connection with transfer of the statutory reserve fund to stated capital (Comm. Code, art. 293–3), stock dividends (Comm. Code, art. 293–2), or stock split (Comm. Code, art. 293–4). If the aggregate amount of par value is fifty million yen or more, notification must be filed with the Ministry of Finance. Registration Rule, art. 8.

offering is nonexistent here, after the transaction has been approved by a shareholders' meeting.

Notification Necessary Where the aggregate par value of shares issued pursuant to the merger agreement is fifty million yen or more, the merging or consolidated corporation is required to file a notification statement with the Ministry of Finance.[5] However, this contributes little to the protection of investors. Financial statements are not components of Form I; thus CPA's audit of the merger balance sheets cannot be expected. Failure to file a notification statement does not affect the validity of a merger, nor does it incur a penal sanction.[6]

There is some doubt about the legality of Registration Rule article 8. The Securities Exchange Law requires notification only where a public offering or secondary distribution is exempt from the registration requirement on account of the small size of the value involved.[7] That the Registration Rule requires notification for a transaction which is neither a public offering nor a secondary distribution seems to exceed the scope of the statutory provision.

Disclosure Measures Once the shareholders' meeting has passed a merger agreement a shareholder can no longer make investment decisions. Consequently, prior disclosure is necessary. The proxy statement, periodic report and other means of continuous disclosure supposedly meet this need. The coverage of these regulations[8] should be reexamined in this context. At the same time attention must be paid to the desirability of replacing them with the registration and prospectus devices.[9]

---

5. Registration Rule, art. 8.

6. SEL, art. 198 item 1 punishes one who has made a public offering or secondary distribution without effective registration. To the extent that an issuance of securities pursuant to merger is construed as not constituting a public offering, the foregoing provision cannot be applied to a violative merger.

7. SEL, art. 4 para. 1 proviso, para. 2. Registration Rule article 4 is based upon this provision.

8. *See* pp. 55–56, 60–61 *supra.*

9. *See* Letter of the Securities and Exchange Commission concerning Rule 133, Securities Act Release No. 3762 (Mar. 15, 1957); Comment, Recent Developments in the No-Sale Theory under the Securities Act of 1933: Proposed Revision of Rule 133, 47 CALIF. L. REV. 112 (1959); DISCLOSURE TO INVESTORS (The Wheat Report) 280–93 (1969).

2. Corporate Reorganization

The Corporate Reorganization Law provides that the registration requirement shall not apply to shares of stock or debentures issued by the corporation or its successor to the creditors, hypothecary obligees or other security holders, or shareholders pursuant to the corporate reorganization plan.[10] This exemption is justified by the fact that the Finance Minister is given an opportunity to express his opinion before the court with regard to the corporate reorganization plan.[11]

3. Convertible Securities

Convertible debentures[12] are not so common as in the United States, and convertible shares[13] are much more rare in Japan. There is no such rule as Rule 155 under the U.S. Securities Act of 1933. If, however, a pseudo-private placement is made for the purpose of concealing a distribution intent, such transaction should be regarded as violative of the registration provision with an intent to evade such requirement.

On the other hand, in the case of convertible securities already registered, the issuance of underlying securities on conversion is free from registration because there is no element of "solicitation," an essential element in public offerings. The issuer is still required to file a notification statement if the aggregate par value of the underlying securities is fifty million yen or more at the time of the issuance.[14]

Where a holder of convertible securities makes a secondary distribution

---

10. *Kaishakōseihō* (Corporate reorganization law), art. 266 (Law No. 172, 1952). The term "reorganization" is used here in its narrow sense, comparable to the procedure stipulated in Chapter X of the U.S. Bankuptcy Act.

11. Corporate Reorganization Law, art. 35 para. 2, art. 232 para. 2. KANEKO AND MIKAZUKI, *Jōkai Kaishakōseihō* (Commentary to the corporate reorganization law) 55 (1955).

12. COMM. CODE, arts. 341–2 through 341–7. The 1966 amendment to the Commercial Code has made it possible for a holder of convertible debentures to convert them into shares of stock even during the period when the shareholder register is closed.

Although still infrequently used, convertible debentures are expected to become more popular in the future. Major securities exchanges have recently decided to list convertible debentures. *See* SHŌKEN (No. 254) 6 (Tokyo Securities Exchange, May 1970).

13. COMM. CODE, arts. 222–2 through 222–7.

14. Registration Rule, art. 8.

of underlying securities after conversion, such distribution is subject to the usual principles governing registration, regardless of whether or not the convertible securities have been registered, since these two types of securities are different.

Chapter 9

Regulation of Securities Companies

1. Licensing Securities Companies

The 1965 amendment to the Securities Exchange Law concerns mainly the regulation of broker-dealers. The term " broker-dealer " (*shōken-gyōsha*) was replaced by " securities company " (*shōken-gaisha*) throughout the law itself and the cabinet and ministerial rules thereunder.

Definitions The term " securities company " is defined as " any stock corporation which has been licensed by the Minister of Finance pursuant to the provision of article 28."[1] Any business organizations other than stock corporations having such license are excluded from managing the securities business.[2] The term " securities business " (*shōkengyō*) is also defined in the law as " any business involved in one of the following activities by any person other than a bank, trust company, or other financial institution designated by a cabinet rule: (a) sale of securities; (b) sale of securities as an intermediary, broker or agent; (c) commissioning of a sale order to be executed on a securities exchange as an intermediary, broker or agent; (d) underwriting of securities; (e) secondary distribution of securities; and (f) arrangement for a public offering or secondary distribution of securities."[3]

Quasi-Segregation Four classes of license are stipulated, and one or more of them should be applied for according to the kind of business the applicant purports to undertake: (1) license for the business of (a) above mentioned; (2) that of (b) and (c); (3) that of (d) and (e); and (4) that of

---

1. SEL, art. 2 para. 9.

2. SEL, art. 28 para. 1. Prior to the 1953 amendment broker-dealers were not confined to stock corporations. A stock corporation (*kabushiki-gaisha*) is provided for in the Commercial Code, articles 165 through 456.

3. SEL, art. 2 para. 8.

(f).[4] Minimum amounts of stated capital are prescribed for the applicant, varying according to the type and location of its business, ranging from three billion to one million yen.[5]

The activities of broker, dealer and underwriter are not segregated, and a given securities company may engage in all of these businesses. To the extent that separate licenses are required in order for a company to engage in more than one kind of business, legislative intent to attain segregation is evidenced here to some degree.[6]

Licensing Standards In granting a license the Finance Minister is required to consider whether the following standards are met: (1) the applicant has sufficient financial status to carry out its proposed business, and the prospect for profits is satisfactory; (2) the applicant, in the light of its personnel, has sufficient knowledge and experience to carry out its business fairly and adequately and has good social standing; (3) the proposed securities business is necessary and appropriate, in the light of

---

4. SEL, art. 28 para. 2.

5. Minimum amounts of stated capital are as follows:

(1) Companies which may engage in underwriting
- a) Managing underwriters who may engage in another kind or kinds of securities business .... 3 billion yen
- b) Managing underwriters who may engage solely in underwriting .... 1 billion yen
- c) Other underwriters .... 200 million yen

(2) Companies which may engage in trading on an exchange market (excluding the foregoing)
- a) Those who may trade on the Tokyo or Osaka exchange .... 100 million yen
- b) Those who may trade on the Nagoya exchange .... 50 million yen
- c) Those who may trade on other exchanges.......... 30 million yen

(3) Companies other than the foregoing
- a) Those who have one or more offices in Tokyo or Osaka...... 30 million yen
- b) Other companies .... 20 million yen

(4) Companies which deal solely with securities companies
- a) Those who have one or more offices in Tokyo or Osaka........4 million yen
- b) Other companies ....1 million yen

SEL, art. 32 para. 1 item 1; SEL Enforcement Rule, art. 3.

Those securities companies which deal solely with other securities companies carry on business within securities exchanges, functioning somewhat like specialists, and are commonly called *saitori* or *nakadachi* members.

6. Regarding the prohibition against a securities company's acting as both broker and dealer in a single sale, *see* p. 76 *infra*. A qualified license (p. 70 *infra*) functions also as a means for segregation.

securities transactions, the number of securities companies and their offices, and other economic circumstances in the district where the applicant purports to carry out its business.[7]

The term "necessary and appropriate" as part of the third criterion above deserves our attention. If construed literally, it would serve to support the maintenance of a monopoly or oligopoly by existing securities companies. Therefore it should be construed in a negative way, to wit, in order to prevent overcompetition among securities companies.[8]

Qualified License The Finance Minister may grant a qualified license if it is necessary in the public interest or for the protection of investors.[9] For example, an applicant purporting to engage in both broker and dealer businesses may be permitted to engage in sales of securities on his own account to the extent necessary to properly effect the customers' orders, or a restriction may be imposed on an underwriter concerning the brands of securities he can deal with or the amount of his holdings.[10]

Background of the 1965 Amendment The criteria for granting a license are considerably abstract and flexible, thus allowing the Finance Minister

---

7. SEL, art. 31. Prior to the 1965 amendment registration was to be refused only where the applicant fell within one of the stipulated disqualifying conditions similar to those of Section 15(5) of the Securities Exchange Act of 1934. A similar provision still exists in the amended law for the refusal of license. SEL, art. 32.

Although the 1965 amendment to the SEL came into force on Oct. 1, 1965, broker-dealers who had been registered in accordance with the provisions prior to the amendment were allowed to continue their business until March 31, 1968, without obtaining a license under the new law. Within this two-and-a-half year period these broker-dealers had to improve their financial and personnel qualifications to meet the new license requirements.

The Ministry of Finance, in response to a request by the securities industry, issued a release designed to clarify the standards for evaluating the application of then-existing securities companies. Ministry of Finance Release (*zōshō*) No. 685, Mar. 23, 1967. This release referred to: (1) financial status and prospect for profit; (2) personnel organization; (3) applicant's violation of any law or rules; (4) miscellaneous. As to point (1) above, the release required that the amount of net assets exceed the amount of stated capital and that the indebtedness ratio (p. 74 *infra*) be ten or less. With the exception of the above, the wording of the release is nonspecific.

8. SUZUKI & KAWAMOTO 90.

9. SEL, art. 29.

10. Miyashita, *Kaisei Shōkentorihikihō Sei-shōrei no Kaisetsu* (Explanation of the amended securities exchange law, cabinet and ministerial rules thereunder), BESSATSU SHŌJI HŌMU KENKYŪ (No. 1) 4 (1965).

broad discretion. The rationale for the change from registration to license is that the latter system is better suited to the climate of Japan, enabling the authorities to keep unsound firms from being established and to execute preventive administration more effectively.[11]

One of the purposes in introducing the licensing system was to obviate the "securities firm bubble" by regulating the sites of securities companies.[12] In fact, more than sixty percent of the registered securities firms had disappeared from the scene.[13] During the transitional stage, dissolutions and mergers of securities firms took place, and 275 licensed securities companies were in operation as of April 1, 1968.[14]

2. Administrative Control

Revocation of a License A license once granted has perpetual duration unless it is revoked by the authorities; therefore there is no need to apply for its renewal. The Minister may revoke or suspend a license in the following cases: (1) where the amount of stated capital of the securities company has decreased to below the statutory minimum, or the company has been convicted of a fine pursuant to the Securities Exchange Law; (2) where the securities company has violated the law, administrative order pursuant to the law, or the qualification attached to the license; (3) where the securities company is on the verge of insolvency and the revocation is indispensable to prevent further losses by investors.[15]

Permit or Approval Securities companies are also subject to administrative control during their existence. A statutory merger, consolidation, transfer or acquisition of all or a part of the business, discontinuance of the business or resolution to dissolve a securities company cannot become effective without a permit from the Finance Minister.[16] A securities company is required to obtain approval from the Minister when it intends to: (a) change its name; (b) change the amount of stated capital; (c)

11. *Id.* at 3.
12. SUZUKI & KAWAMOTO 88.
13. Between 1948 and 1964 the total number of registered securities firms amounted to 1,567, of which 1,034 firms had their registration revoked or written off, mainly because of financial distress. 1968 MOF ANN. REP. 25.
14. 1968 MOF ANN. REP. 24.
15. SEL, art. 35.
16. SEL, art. 34.

change its policy of conducting business; (d) set up a branch or other office; (e) change the location of its principal or other office; or (f) alter the status of its office to a branch.[17] Several other matters are also to be reported to the Minister without delay.[18]

A securities company is prohibited from engaging in a business other than that of securities except such business as approved by the Finance Minister.[19] Full-time directors are also forbidden to engage in a daily business for other companies or in their own business without the Minister's approval.[20]

Correction Order The Finance Minister has the power to order correction of the business or finance policy of a securities company where he considers it necessary and appropriate in the public interest or for the protection of investors.[21] The correction order shall prescribe alteration of method of business, suspension of all or a part of the business for a period not exceeding three months, escrow of assets, or other matters necessary for his supervision.

---

17. SEL, art. 33. A " branch " (*shiten*) is usually distinguished from " other office " in that the former has a certain measure of autonomy, whereas the latter is wholly subject to directions given by the principal office or a branch.

18. SEL, art. 37. (1) Where there has been a change in directors or auditors; (2) where the company has been fined pursuant to the SEL, or a director or auditor of the company has been declared bankrupt or convicted with imprisonment or fine; (3) where the company has discontinued its approved side business; (4) where the company has suspended or reopened its business; (5) where the company has abolished its office or changed a branch into a non-branch office.

19. SEL, art. 43. The side business to be approved must pertain to securities. Important was the so-called " investment deposit " (*un'yō-azukari*) whereby a securities company borrowed securities (especially financial notes) for consideration from unspecified many persons and used the securities as collaterals. Nineteen companies were given approval to engage in this type of business. In 1965 the aggregate value of securities thus deposited reached its maximum, 265 billion yen. In the same year, the financial difficulties of securities companies due to the recession led to a run on those companies. The authorities decided to withhold approval of this type of side business. Ministry of Finance Release (*zōshō*) No. 1879, Oct. 9, 1967. 1969 MOF ANN. REP. 142–43.

At present, important side businesses include installment investment (*ruisekitōshi*), agency activities regarding debt securities (receiving payment for them, paying out principal and interest), safety deposit and so on. Some companies were given approval to act as investment advisors. 1969 MOF ANN. REP. 146–47; SUZUKI & KAWAMOTO 114–15.

20. SEL, art. 42.

21. SEL, art. 54 para. 1. The Soundness Rule (p. 74 *infra*) details the circumstances under which a correction order may be issued.

3. Maintenance of Financial Soundness

One of the chief purposes of the 1965 amendment was to keep securities companies financially sound, in order to protect public investors against damages from insolvency of the company with which they might be dealing.

Reserves to Be Accumulated Securities companies are required to accumulate three kinds of reserve funds. (1) Revenue reserve (*rieki-jumbikin*). A securities company must set aside at least one-fifth of its cash dividends at each fiscal period until such revenue reserve reaches an amount equal to that of the stated capital.[22] This reserve may not be used otherwise than for writing off the deficit.[23] (2) Sales loss reserve (*baibai sonshitsu jumbikin*). A certain portion of the surplus of profits derived from sales of securities over losses derived likewise should be set aside for this reserve fund, which may be used only for writing off deficits caused by sales of securities except with approval by the Finance Minister.[24] This requirement concerns securities companies engaged in dealer activities. (3) Securities transaction liability reserve (*shōkentorihiki sekinin jumbikin*). This reserve fund must be accumulated by a securities company in proportion to the volume of securities transactions, in order to meet the liability borne by the company as a result of securities trouble.[25] This is not a completely new kind of reserve fund, but has been accumulated by securities companies

---

22. SEL, art. 57. Every stock corporation must accumulate a revenue reserve——but amounting to only one-tenth of the cash dividends until the total reaches one-fourth of the stated capital. COMM. CODE, art. 288. The new requirement for securities companies is equivalent to that for banks. *Ginkōhō* (Banking law), art. 8 (Law No. 21, 1927).

23. COMM. CODE, art. 289.

24. SEL, art. 56. The method of calculation is prescribed in the Securities Company Rule, art. 7–2.

25. SEL, art. 57–2. As a rule, the amount to be set aside is 0.03 yen per share involved in sales or brokerage transactions. Securities Company Rule, art. 8. Most of the shares have a par value of 50 yen, and where the market price is 50 yen or lower the ordinary brokerage commission is 1.30 yen per share for an order involving less than five thousand Shares.

" Securities trouble " (*shōkenjiko*) is defined as " an illegal or undue act committed by an officer or an employee of a securities company as to sales of securities or other transactions, and which has caused or may cause a dispute between the company and its customer." *Sozei Tokubetsusochihō Shikōrei* (Special tax measure law enforcement rule), art. 33 para. 1 (Cabinet Rule No. 32, 1957).

pursuant to a provision in constitutions of securities firm associations and recognized by the tax authority as eligible to be credited in an expense account.[26]

Indebtedness Ratio In cases where the business or financial status of a securities company tends to be unsound, the Finance Minister may issue a correction order. Among the stipulated circumstances in which the business or financial status is judged unsound, excessive indebtedness is an important consideration. The ratio is calculated by dividing aggregate indebtedness (including long-term debts) by net assets (regardless of the liquidity).[27] If this ratio exceeds or tends to exceed ten, financial unsoundness may be presumed.[28] This ratio is different from that of the United States.[29] The reason for this alteration has been explained as follows: " Since broker-dealers are confined to stock corporations and prohibited from engaging in another business, there is no need to distinguish the business assets. Under the former rule which included only current assets and debts with a formal criterion of one year, modification of the ratio without recovery of substantial solvency was easily made and reduced the effectiveness of the rule."[30]

Standards of Soundness The Ministry of Finance has set up " Standards of Soundness; " if the conduct of a securities company does not meet these standards the Finance Minister may issue a correction order. The standards are as follows:

(1) Securities held in the account of the securities company itself

---

26. The SEL does not stipulate how this reserve should be maintained. The tax authority requires, as a condition for crediting it in an expense account, that the reserve shall be deposited in cash with the securities firm association. *Sozei Tokubetsusochihō* (Special tax measure law), art. 57 (Law No. 26, 1957). Every month securities companies deposit with the association the amount calculated pursuant to Securities Company Rule art. 8. SUZUKI & KAWAMOTO 131.

27. SEL, art. 54 para. 1 item 1, para. 2; SEL Enforcement Rule, art. 4.

28. Securities Company Rule, art. 6.

29. Rule 15c 3–1, 17 C.F.R. § 240. 15c3–1. Before the 1965 amendment, Japanese law substantially followed this rule.

30. Miyashita, *supra* note 10, at 8.

The requirement that the indebtedness ratio shall not exceed ten is a very generous one. The present rule took into consideration the fact that the financial status of securities companies is low compared with that of average corporations. SUZUKI & KAWAMOTO 119–22.

shall be limited to the minimum amount necessary to do business, and shall be diversified into many brands and into liquid form.

(2) Loans, advances and loan securities shall be restricted to those which are necessary to do business, and their amounts, periods, collaterals and other conditions shall be reasonable.

(3) As to deposits, debts and borrowed securities, their amounts, periods, interest and other conditions shall not be unsound in the light of the financial situation of the company.

(4) As to securities deposited from customers, the amount shall not be excessive and these securities shall be kept surely and orderly in safe facilities.

(5) As to fixed business assets, their amount shall be within adequate limitation in comparison with the amount of net assets, and their size, structure and equipments shall be reasonable in the light of business, the number of employees and location.[31]

31. SEL, art. 54 para. 1 item 2; Soundness Rule, art. 2. Standard (1) is based on the fact that securities companies held too many shares in their own account, a practice which amplified the effect of a market fall. SUZUKI & KAWAMOTO 124–25. As shown in the following table, dealer transactions outweighed broker transactions in 1963 and 1964. Big securities companies took the initiative in the "go public" movement of medium-sized corporations until the market decline in July 1963, which led to the business failure of Yamaichi Securities Company. After the promulgation of the Soundness Rule, the average position of securities companies gradually improved.

Stock Trading Volume by All Securities Companies on Exchanges (million shares)

Fiscal year	Total	Broker basis	%	Dealer basis
1960	86,229	40,838	47.4	45,392
1961	113,410	54,581	48.1	58,830
1962	100,345	52,638	52.5	47,662
1963	136,095	67,681	49.7	68,415
1964	87,502	43,594	49.8	43,908
1965	88,995	48,791	54.8	40,203
1966	110,649	64,734	58.5	45,915
1967	90,835	54,436	59.9	36,399
1968	119,650	79,088	66.1	40,562

1968 MOF ANN. REP. Table 114 at 171; 1969 MOF ANN. REP. Table 124 at 141. The fiscal year of a securities company begins on October 1 and ends on September 30. SEL, art. 52. Fiscal year 1960 refers to the period between October 1, 1959, and September 30, 1960.

4. Protection of Customers

Broker or Dealer? When a securities company receives an order from a customer, the company must inform him in advance as to whether it acts on its own account or effects the order for his account,[32] and the company is prohibited from acting as both dealer and broker with regard to a single sale of securities.[33] This represents one of the steps taken toward the segregation of securities businesses. As broker, the securities company must abide by the customer's limited order.[34] A securities company is required to send a sales confirmation to its customer without delay after conclusion of the transaction.[35] There is a restriction on hypothecation of customers' securities.[36]

Prohibited Fraudulent Acts In addition to these restrictions and the regulation on financial conditions and registered representatives, the law prohibits securities companies, their officers and employees from engaging in certain fraudulent activities: (1) soliciting orders by giving an affirmative judgment that the price of the security will rise or fall; (2) soliciting orders with the aid of a promise that the company will compensate all or a part of the customer's loss; (3) making false or misleading representations in connection with a transaction; (4) soliciting orders with the aid of a promise to offer certain benefits; (5) effecting a series of transactions creating manipulative quotations, or entrusting or knowingly to be entrusted to effect such transactions (regardless of the purpose of inducing the purchase or sale by others); (6) settling the company's own balance derived from its counter-sale against the customer's margin transaction by another counter-sale; (7) an officer or employee taking advantage of special information obtained through his position for selling or purchasing securities or solely for the purpose of lucrative speculation.[37]

---

32. SEL, art. 46.
33. SEL, arts. 47 and 129.
34. COMM. CODE, art. 554.
35. SEL, art. 48.
36. SEL, art. 51.
37. SEL, art. 50; Soundness Rule, art. 1. There exists a general anti-fraud provision, SEL, art. 58, which was modeled after Section 17 of the 1933 Act and Section 10 (b) of the 1934 Act of the United States. Unlike the American model, SEL art. 58 is a self-contained provision. However, it has not been utilized as often as its counterpart in the United States, due mainly to its abstract wording. This is why SEL article 50 and the rule thereunder were introduced in the 1965 amendment.

Registered Representatives Before the 1965 amendment there was no provision on registered representatives except that which required a securities company to notify the Finance Minister of names and other identification items of such registered representatives.[38] Regulation was entrusted to associations of securities firms. Under such circumstances a number of cases arose where registered representatives appropriated customers' money or securities, or registered representative made transactions on customers' accounts without instructions. The majority of courts, including the Supreme Court, held that the employer securities company was liable for the misconduct of an employee registered representative, on the ground of the existence of actual authority,[39] apparent authority,[40] or employer's torts liability.[41] However, a few courts denied relief for the customer on the theory that the registered representative was an agent not of the securities company but of the customer.[42] This confusion derived primarily from the fact that many registered representatives (and almost all of those involved in the cases mentioned above) live solely on commission without any fixed salary and retain their own customers even after they have changed from one employer securities company to another.[43] This fact, however, does not justify the immunity of the employer securities companies, since

---

38. SEL, art. 56 (before the 1965 amendment).

39. Mikami v. Eguchi Shōken K.K., 17 Minshū 1596 (Sup. Ct., 3d Petty Bench, Dec. 3, 1963); Homma v. Nippon Sangyō Shōken K.K., HANREI JIHŌ (No.242) 30 (Tokyo Dist. Ct., May 6, 1960); Furukawa v. Gōdō Shōken K.K., 7 Kakyū minshū 3271 (Tokyo Dist. Ct., Nov. 16, 1956).

40. CIVIL CODE, arts. 109 and 110 (Law No. 89, 1896). Under pre-war legislation which permitted independent intermediaries, some courts relied on the principle of apparent authority.

41. CIVIL CODE, art. 715. Uchida v. Nichiei Shōken K.K. *et al.*, HANREI JIHŌ (No. 337) 39 (Tokyo Dist. Ct., May 13, 1963).

42. Sato v. Nippon Shōken K.K., 6 Kakyū minshū 2340 (Osaka Dist. Ct., Nov. 8, 1955) (the customer did not have a regular receipt to be issued by the company); Kubota v. Tokyo Shin'ei Shōken K.K., 4 Kakyū minshū 180 (Tokyo Dist. Ct., Feb. 2, 1953) (the customer entrusted the registered representative as an individual); Hosoda v. Nippon Kangyō Shōken K.K., HANREI TAIMUZU (No. 50) 55 (Tokyo High Ct., June 29, 1955).

43. These commission registered representatives (*buai-gaimuin*) exceeded sixty percent in 1953, but dwindled to thirty-eight percent in 1961. OSAKA SHŌKENGYŌKYŌKAI (Osaka Association of Securities Firms) *Zoku Shōken Jūnenshi* (A decade of securities) 146 (Supp. 1961). The Labor Standards Law was held inapplicable to this class of registered representatives. Ishihara v. Yamasaki Shōken K.K., 15 Minshū 1322 (Sup. Ct., 1st Petty Bench. May 25, 1961).

customers rely on the reputation of these companies and employers take advantage of business expansion owing to their registered representatives.[44]

The 1965 amendment purported to clear up this problem and to tighten the control on registered representatives. A securities company is required to register with the Finance Minister every officer or employee who engages in the business outside the offices of the company.[45] The Finance Minister may refuse, revoke or suspend such registration on certain grounds.[46] A registered representative is deemed to be authorized to perform on behalf of the securities company to which he belongs all extrajudicial acts relating to securities transactions except where the other party has been in bad faith.[47] It is expected that this express provision will reduce the number of lawsuits brought against securities companies which denied their liability on the ground of unauthorized conduct by registered representatives.

5. Association of Securities Firms

Federalism After the model of the Maloney Act,[48] the Securities Exchange Law provides for registration and regulation of securities firm associations.[49] Unlike the NASD, however, there are ten such associations in Japan.[50] These associations comprise the Japan Federation of Securities Firm Associations (*Nippon Shōkengyōkyōkai Rengōkai*).[51]

---

44. Yazawa, 3 *Tōdai Shōjihanrei Kenkyū* (Tokyo University, Comments on commercial cases) 296 (1952); *id.* vol. 6, at 374 (1955).

45. SEL, art. 62.

46. SEL. arts. 63 and 64–3.

47. SEL, art. 64.

"(1) A registered representative shall be deemed as having the authority to perform any extrajudicial acts with regard to the sale or purchase and other transactions of securities on behalf of the securities company to which he belongs.

(2) The provision of the foregoing paragraph shall be inapplicable where the other party has acted in bad faith."

"Other transactions" include the receipt of securities or money from a customer for the sale or purchase of securities, the receipt of securities from a customer for safe deposit or registration on the shareholder register, and the receipt of money for subscription of shares on behalf of the customer. Suzuki & Kawamoto 140–41; Mikami v. Eguchi Shōken K.K., *supra* note 39. "Bad faith" means that the customer has been actually cognizant of the fact that the registered representative has acted without authority.

48. Securities Exchange Act of 1934, sec. 15 A, 15 U.S.C.A. § 78 *o*-3.

49. SEL, arts. 67 through 79.

50. Thirty-three associations of securities firms used to exist in Japan, averaging nearly

Membership Securities companies are not statutorily obliged to join the association of securities firms, although, in fact, all securities companies are members with the exception of *saitori* or *nakadachi* who, like the " specialist " in the United States, trade only with other security companies on the floor.[52]

As a result of the multiplicity of associations, there are two types of membership: principal office members and branch members. Principal office members have some priority over branch members as to management of the association, notwithstanding the fact that the latter outnumber and outweigh in trading volume the former in local associations.[53]

The advantage of membership in a securities firm association is not so marked as in the case of NASD, since members are not prohibited from dealing with non-member broker-dealers at a discount rate.[54] But securities exchanges stipulate in their Entrustment Contract Regulations that members of exchanges shall collect from members of a securities firm

---

one in each prefecture. The Securities Counseling Commission suggested in its report of Feb. 12, 1964, that in order to achieve more effective self-regulation the multiplicity of associations should be replaced by a new national association of securities firms. In its report of Dec. 22, 1964, the Commission stressed the need to incorporate such a national association and to tighten administrative control thereof. In addition, the Commission advocated as a mandatory requirement that all securities companies be members of the association.

From 1965 to 1967 the Japan Federation of Securities Firm Associations and local associations made a study of their future organization and functions, and formulated the following policies:

(1) Thirty-three associations should be integrated into ten associations through merger and consolidation.

(2) The charter of the Japan Federation of Securities Firm Associations should be amended to strengthen the controlling power of the Federation over local associations to require local associations to prescribe and enforce their rules and regulations according to the suggestions of the Federation.

(3) In the future, a new national association of securities firms should be established to replace the existing Federation, and local associations should become the branches of the new national association.

Following these policies, the Japan Federation of Securities Firms Associations amended its charter on April 19, 1968, and thirty-three local associations were integrated into ten new associations of securities firms on May 1, 1968. 1968 MOF ANN. REP. 236–38.

51. The federation itself is to be registered with the Finance Ministry. SEL, art. 79.

52. *See* p. 69 note 5 *supra*.

53. Shōkentorihikihō Kenkyūkai, IMBESUTOMENTO 7 (special ed. 1965).

54. *Cf.* SECURITIES EXCHANGE ACT OF 1934, sec. 15 A (i) (1), 15 U.S.C.A. § 78 *o*-3 (i) (1).

association a sum equal to half the amount of commissions they charge customers in general.[55]

Self-Regulation Self-regulation by associations is less active than in the case of NASD. Associations have never taken the initiative in expelling members, but have expelled only those members whose registration as broker-dealers has been revoked by the authority or who have been expelled from certain securities exchange.[56] The national federation of such associations is concerned mainly with petitioning the government and the Diet, promoting public relations as to securities investment, instructing its member associations as to rules and regulations and arbitrating disputes between members of different associations, especially as to the establishment of offices.

In short, securities firm associations in Japan are interest groups of securities companies rather than self-regulatory organizations. Strong and active associations cannot be expected to grow in a climate where the over-the-counter market is quite inactive.[57]

---

55. *E.g.*, Tokyo Securities Exchange, Entrustment Contract Regulations (*jutakukeiyaku junsoku*), Table 1, I (2).

Members of a securities firm association used to be entitled to participation in a public offering or secondary distribution managed by a fellow member. *Kabushikikōkai ni kansuru Kisoku* (Rule concerning public offering of stock) (Uniform Practice Code No. 6). Members earned much from this privilege when hot issues were made, especially during the "go public" movement. This privilege was abolished as of April 1968 on the ground that it did not conform to the 1965 amendment which introduced licensing of a securities company according to its type of business. In other words, those securities companies which do not have a license to engage in underwriting are not entitled to participation in a public offering. 1968 MOF ANN. REP. 241.

56. Shōkentorihikihō Kenkyūkai, *supra* note 53, at 18.

57. Each association of securities firms has its own Rules of Fair Practice and Uniform Practice Code. These are meager, however, in comparison with those of the NASD, mainly because of the lesser importance of the over-the-counter market in Japan. SUZUKI & KAWAMOTO 180. As to the recent movement for integration, *see supra* note 50.

CHAPTER 10

Securities Exchanges

1. Organization and Regulation

There are eight securities exchanges in Japan—Tokyo, Osaka, Nagoya, Kyoto, Fukuoka, Hiroshima, Niigata and Sapporo—the first two of which are outstanding in their volume of trade.[1]

License for Formation In order to establish a securities exchange, a license must be obtained from the Finance Minister,[2] who may refuse to grant a license not only where the applicant falls within one of the disqualifying conditions[3] but also where the rules and regulations, organization or economic circumstances of the applicant's location are not considered as meeting the standards stipulated by law.[4] Once granted, a license is perpetual unless revoked by the Minister or withdrawn by virtue of dissolution of the exchange.

Administrative Control A permit from the Finance Minister must be obtained for an amendment to the constitution, rules or regulations of a securities exchange.[5] The Minister is also authorized to order an amend-

---

1. In 1968 each exchange contributed the following portion in volume of shares of stock traded on all exchanges: Tokyo (68.7%), Osaka (23.0%), Nagoya (3.1%), Kyoto (0.5%), Hiroshima (0.5%), Fukuoka (0.2%), Niigata (0.3%), Sapporo (0.1%). 1969 MOF ANN. REP. Table 7 at 324–25.

Nine securities exchanges were in operation prior to the dissolution of the Kobe Securities Exchange on October 31, 1967. The share in trading volume of the Tokyo Securities Exchange has gradually increased, while that of other exchanges has decreased. Stock trading is concentrated in Tokyo and Osaka, and local exchanges are losing their traditional function. SUZUKI & KAWAMOTO 146.

2. SEL, art. 81 para. 2. The 1953 amendment substituted a license for a registration in order to prevent the establishment of an excessive number of exchanges.

3. SEL, art. 83 para. 2.

4. SEL, art. 83 para. 1.

5. SEL, art. 85–2 para. 1.

ment to these rules.[6] He has power to inspect exchanges[7] and, if he finds some violation of law, rules or administrative orders, may revoke or suspend the license, or remove the officers of the exchange.[8]

Securities Market There is no statutory provision for exempted exchanges.[9] A " securities market " is, by definition, limited to that which a licensed exchange furnishes for the purpose of securities sales.[10] It is prohibited to establish a facility similar to a securities market or to trade on such facility.[11] This prohibition was inherited from the pre-war law,[12] and courts held thereunder that a place or facility on which many buyers and sellers traded systematically through certain intermediaries fell within the compass of such " similar facility," even in cases where the place consisted of several distant spots or traders did not actually gather.[13] According to this view telephone markets should be banned. Under present law, however, there is no precedent in this respect. The collective over-the-counter trading effected at the offices of intermediaries, suspected to be in contravention of this provision, was absorbed by " floor section II " in the Tokyo, Osaka and Nagoya exchanges.[14]

---

6. SEL, art. 156.

7. SEL, art. 154.

8. SEL, art. 155 item 1.

The Securities Counseling Commission published a report " On the Improvement of Facilities for Stock Trading " on July 10, 1967. The Commission pointed out that the management of securities exchanges was not always carried out in the public interest and for the protection of investors. It was urged that non-member directors be increased and the power of the president be extended. 1968 MOF ANN. REP. 250–51. Securities exchanges effected reforms along these lines. 1969 MOF ANN. REP. 172–75.

9. *Cf.* SECURITIES EXCHANGE ACT OF 1934, sec. 5 (2), 15 U.S.C.A. § 78 e (2).

10. SEL, art. 2 paras. 11 and 12.

11. SEL, art. 191.

12. Exchange Law of 1893, art. 26–2.

13. Hiroumi v. Gōshigaisha Daigo Shōten, 24 Minroku 2053 (Great Ct. of Cassation, 3d Civil Dept., Oct. 23, 1918) ; Japan v. the accused, 6 Keishū 72 (Great Ct. of Cassation, 3d Criminal Dept., Mar. 5, 1927) ; Japan v. Nishimura *et al.*, HŌRITSU SHIMBUN (No. 2710) 9 (Great Ct. of Cassation, 6th Criminal Dept., April 8, 1927). These cases were criticized in academic circles.

14. No over-the-counter market of considerable significance exists in Japan, whereas many securities of big issuers are traded in the over-the-counter market in the United States. This is due partly to the provision forbidding the establishment of, and tradings on, facilities similar to securities exchanges. It is true that there are a tremendous number of unlisted corporations, but most of them are " family corporations " of small size, their shares of stock being rarely transferred. In 1961 when collective tradings in some

2. Members and Discipline

Member Corporation Membership in a securities exchange is confined to securities companies.[15] Consequently a securities exchange consists exclusively of corporate members and membership by an individual is impossible. A member corporation effects transactions on the floor by its floor representatives, traders and floor assistants.[16]

Discipline by the Exchange The constitution of a securities exchange must include provision for a member's expulsion or suspension, or imposition of a fine upon him, for conduct in contravention of law, administrative orders or rules of the exchange, or inconsistent with just and equitable principles of trade.[17] Accordingly, each securities exchange provides a wide range of disciplinary rules. Aside from the suspension of membership, an exchange may suspend all or part of the privilege of a member to conduct tradings on the exchange.

Discipline by the Government While the SEC is authorized to suspend or expel from a national securities exchange any member or officer thereof who has committed a misconduct,[18] the Finance Minister is not authorized

---

unlisted stocks developed to such a point that the markets began to assume the characteristics of quasi-exchanges and doubts arose as to their legality in the light of article 191, the Tokyo, Osaka and Nagoya securities exchanges, acting upon the instruction of the Ministry of Finance, absorbed these markets in their newly built " floor section II," with less stringent listing standards. Consequently it is a distinct characteristic of the Japanese securities market that almost all securities transactions are made on securities exchanges.

15. SEL, art. 90. Securities exchanges stipulate in their constitution that a member shall be a securities company incorporated pursuant to Japanese law, that a member shall not be under control of an alien or foreign corporation, and that the board of directors of the exchange shall set criteria whereby control of an alien is to be determined. *E.g.*, Tokyo Securities Exchange, Constitution, art. 8 ; Osaka Securities Exchange, Constitution, art. 8.

16. In the case of the Tokyo Securities Exchange, each member has two floor representatives and such number of traders and floor assistants as determined according to the member's volume of trading and amount of stated capital. The Osaka Securities Exchange recognizes only one floor representative per member.

17. SEL, art. 98. *Cf.* SECURITIES EXCHANGE ACT OF 1934, sec. 6 (b), 15 U.S.C.A. § 78 f (b).

18. SECURITIES EXCHANGE ACT OF 1934, sec. 19 (a) (3), 15 U.S.C.A. § 78 s (a) (3).

to do so but must resort instead to indirect enforcement, namely, a threat to revoke or suspend the license of an exchange which fails to discipline its members.[19] On the other hand, the Minister may revoke the license of such a member corporation,[20] and a member deprived of its license as a securities company necessarily loses its membership. Therefore the actual difference between the two practices is not so great as it may appear.

3. Listing and Delisting

Procedures As a rule, the listing of a security is made by the exchange, on application of the issuer of the security, in accordance with the listing standards, and with the approval of the Finance Minister.[21] There is no provision on unlisted trading privileges,[22] but some of the small local exchanges have listed certain securities without an application by the issuer. Multiple listing is common in Japan, and big issuers apply for listing to more than one, very often to all, of the eight exchanges. An exchange may delist a security in accordance with the delisting standards, again with the approval of the Minister.[23] An issuer may request delisting, with the Minister's approval, against the exchange which declines to delist the security.[24]

Supervision over Listed Corporations Listed corporations, except those which file a periodic report with the Finance Minister, are required to file a periodic report on listed securities with the exchange within three months after the expiration of each accounting period.[25] A securities exchange

---

19. SEL, art. 155 item 1.
20. SEL, art. 35.
21. SEL, art. 110. In addition the Minister may order an exchange to list the additional new stock of an issuer whose shares are already listed on the exchange. SEL, art. 111.

The Securities Exchange Law at its outset adopted the dualistic requirements of registration and listing of securities with securities exchanges, following the American model. SEL, arts. 110 through 112 (before the 1953 amendment). *Cf.* SECURITIES EXCHANGE ACT OF 1934, sec. 12 (a) through 12 (e), 15 U.S.C.A. § 78 *l* (a) through (e). The 1953 amendment, however, abolished the requirement of registering securities with exchanges, and at present the only requirement for trading a security on an exchange is that of listing.

22. *Cf.* SECURITIES EXCHANGE ACT OF 1934, sec. 12 (f), 15 U.S.C.A. § 78 *l* (f).
23. SEL, art. 112.
24. SEL, art. 113.
25. SEL, art. 118. *See also* p. 56 *supra*.

is authorized to suspend trading of a listed security, and the Finance Minister must be notified without delay.[26] The Minister may order an exchange to delist or suspend certain listed securities after giving the issuer appropriate notice and opportunity for hearing.[27]

Exemptions Provisions on listing are not applicable to national government bonds, local government bonds, notes issued by a corporation pursuant to a specific statute (financial notes and bonds guaranteed by the government), certificates of contribution issued by a corporation organized pursuant to a specific statute, and foreign national government bonds and foreign local government bonds.[28] In other words, securities exchanges may list and delist such securities without approval of the Finance Minister.

Transferability of Stock In connection with the 1966 amendment to the Commercial Code which enabled a corporation to impose a restriction on transfer of its stock,[29] securities exchanges have amended their listing standards to include a requirement of transferability of stock without restriction.[30]

---

26. SEL, art. 117.
27. SEL, art. 119.
28. SEL, art. 120; SEL Enforcement Rule, art. 7.
29. COMM. CODE, arts. 204 through 204–5.
30. All securities exchanges amended their listing standards and delisting standards in July–August 1966. The new provisions on standards, in exactly the same wording, state that a listed corporation may not restrict the transferability of its shares. However, where a corporation established pursuant to the special statute restricts the transfer of its stock according to the provision in that statute, and this restriction does not obstruct trading of the shares on the floor, the securities exchange may approve the listing of such stocks. *E.g.*, Tokyo Securities Exchange, Listing Standard, art. 4 item 9 (1); Delisting Standard, art. 2 item 9. This proviso is applicable to such corporations as the Japan Airlines Corporation established according to the Law on Japan Airlines Corporation.

Before enforcement of the 1966 amendment to the Commercial Code, it was officially explained that the purpose of the newly added art. 204–2 was to give closely-held corporations a legal means to protect themselves from striking shareholders by refusing approval on a proposed transfer of shares to the shareholders. After that amendment, however, business circles and the Expert Committee of the Foreign Capital Counseling Commission insisted that listed corporations should be permitted to make use of the stock transfer restriction in order to prevent a takeover by foreign corporations. Although there was much discussion of this problem, securities exchanges have not as yet changed their policy.

4. Floor Trading

Administration of the Market Transactions by members on an exchange are controlled primarily by the Business Regulations adopted by the exchange with the Finance Minister's approval.[31] In addition to his power to issue orders in case of violation by an exchange, its members or issuers, the Minister is authorized, if in his opinion the condition of trading on the exchange is harmful to the public interest or for the protection of investors, to suspend all or part of the trading on the exchange for a period not exceeding ten days, or, with cabinet approval, to suspend all or a part of the business of the exchange for a period not exceeding three months.[32]

Sales Contract and Liquidation Trading in certain specified brands of stock, at the beginning and end of each session, is conducted through a modified form of auction by exchange employees. Other trading is made by individual match of bid and offer, through the hands of members of a special class—*saitori* members in Tokyo and *nakadachi* members in Osaka.[33] Most exchange transactions, including all regular and when-issued transactions, are settled through the clearing department of the exchange.[34]

---

31. SEL, art. 108, art. 82 para. 2, art. 85–2 para. 1.

32. SEL, art. 155 para. 1 item 2.

33. *E.g.*, Tokyo Securities Exchange, *Gyōmukitei* (Business regulations), arts. 11, 12 and 29. Osaka Securities Exchange, Business Regulations, arts. 11, 12 and 29. As for *saitori* or *nakadachi* members, *see* p. 69 note 5 *supra*.

34. Osaka Securities Exchange, Business Regulations, art. 46. The Tokyo Securities Exchange requires that all transactions be liquidated through its clearing department. Tokyo Securities Exchange, Business Regulations, art. 46. Unlike exchanges in the United States, Japanese exchanges contain their own clearing departments.

In December 1967 the Tokyo Securities Exchange initiated the central clearing of securities in the area of warrants transaction. The Japan Securities Clearing Corporation, a wholly owned subsidiary of the Tokyo Securities Exchange, deals as the bookkeeping corporation, with the delivery of warrants among clearing members, and with subscription of and payment for new shares using warrants on behalf of clearing members, etc. As this corporation has branch offices in Osaka and Nagoya, settlement among Tokyo, Osaka and Nagoya can be cleared through this system. Tokyo Securities Exchange, 1968 *Shōken Nenkan* (Annual report on securities) 168–72. It is expected that in the future this system will cover all tradings on the floor.

Trading Unit Since the par value of most stocks is as low as fifty yen,[35] the minimum unit for trading is fixed by exchanges. A unit is 1,000 shares on floor section I and 500 shares on floor section II, but if par value is five hundred yen or higher the unit is 100 shares on both floors; as for debt securities, a par value of one hundred thousand yen constitutes a unit.[36]

5. Manipulation and Stabilization

Manipulation In order to maintain a free market for securities, the Securities Exchange Law prohibits certain activities with respect to listed securities: (1) washed sales;[37] (2) matched orders;[38] (3) to entrust or be entrusted with the above;[39] (4) manipulation in the narrow sense, i.e., a series of transactions to change the market price, and entrustment thereof;[40] (5) statements that the market price of the security will be changed by manipulation;[41] and (6) willful misrepresentation.[42]

This prohibition was introduced after the American model.[43] However, the Japanese provisions mentioned above have not been applied for more than two decades. The reason for this is that it is very difficult to prove the "purpose" of the party concerned.[44] As to (1) through (3) above, the "purpose of creating a misleading appearance of active trading in the security, or a misleading appearance with respect to the market for the security" must be proved. As to (4) through (6) above, the "purpose of inducing the purchase or sale of the security by others" must be established.

The SEC of the United States copes with this difficulty by resorting to circumstantial evidence. The extensive stock watch system makes this possible. The Ministry of Finance, however, has no comparable watch system, making it hard to collect circumstantial evidence. Instead, the

35. *See* p. 14 note 37 *supra.*

36. Tokyo Securities Exchange, Business Regulations, art. 14; Osaka Securities Exchange, Business Regulations, art. 14.

37. SEL, art. 125 para. 1 item 1.

38. SEL, art. 125 para. 1 items 2 and 3.

39. SEL, art. 125 para. 1 item 4.

40. SEL, art. 125 para. 2 item 1.

41. SEL, art. 125 para. 2 item 2.

42. SEL, art. 125 para. 2 item 3.

43. Securities Exchange Act of 1934, sec. 9(a), 15 U.S.C.A. § 78*i*(a).

44. Suzuki & Kawamoto 236.

Ministry has resorted to the Soundness Rule, thus avoiding the need for proof of purpose.[45] On this ground, however, the Finance Minister can only issue an administrative order, whereas violation of the anti-manipulation provision incurs civil liabilities as well as penal sanctions.[46]

Stabilization It is prohibited for any person to conduct either alone or with one or more other persons any series of transactions for the purchase or sale of any security on a securities market, or to entrust or to be entrusted to do the same, for the purpose of pegging, fixing or stabilizing the price of such security in contravention to the cabinet rule.[47] The Stabilization Rule[48] prescribes notification, price limit and disclosure with regard to a stabilization facilitating a public offering or secondary distribution.

A conflict of views exists as to whether it is legal or not to stabilize the price of a security in cases other than a public offering or secondary distribution, e.g., for the purpose of maintaining the value of a security as collateral.[49] Literal interpretation of the provision may lead to the argument that such act is legal, a questionable conclusion in the light of investor protection.

To date, only two notifications have been filed with the Finance Minister pursuant to the Stabilization Rule.[50] This fact suggests that the Rule has not been enforced effectively, here again due mainly to the weakness of the stock watch system.

---

45. *Id.* at 240. Soundness Rule, art. 1 item 3: "A series of sales or purchases or entrustment thereof which is likely to create an artificial market price deviating from the actual market, or the act of being entrusted with a series of sales or purchases with the knowledge that an artificial market price deviating from the actual market is likely to be created."

46. SEL, arts. 126, 197 item 2.

47. SEL, art. 125 para. 3.

48. *Anteisōsa ni kansuru Kisoku* (Rule concerning stabilization) (Securities Exchange Commission Rule No. 18, 1948).

49. Suzuki & Kawamoto 238–39.

50. *Id.* at 240.

Chapter 11

Sales and Transfer of Stock

1. Sales Orders

So-called " Swallowing " By virtue of the overwhelming predominance of the exchange market as against the over-the-counter market, most sales orders deal with listed securities of which a large portion are shares of stock. When a securities company which is an exchange member accepts a sell or buy order to be effected on the exchange market, it is illegal for the company to conclude the sales contract by acting as a dealer without executing the order on the exchange market.[1] This practice is commonly called " swallowing " (*nomikōi*) and has been prohibited since pre-war times. In those days when future transactions prevailed, " swallowing " usually meant a contest between the firm and its customer in that the firm bought whenever the customer gave an order to sell, and vice versa.[2] Today the purpose of such prohibition may primarily be found in the necessity to concentrate tradings in the exchange market.[3] On the other hand, if a customer offers to buy or sell instead of giving an order to be effected on exchange market, it is not illegal for the firm to conclude a sales contract on its own account with the customer, even in cases where the sale concerns a listed security.[4] It is not always clear, however, whether a sales contract or an entrustment contract for sale is concluded between a securities company and its customer.[5]

1. SEL, art. 129 para. 1. The securities exchange is obligated to take disciplinary action against such member. SEL, art. 129 para. 2. A similar prohibition applicable to over-the-counter market is prescribed in SEL, art. 47.

2. Fujita 271.

3. Suzuki & Kawamoto 247.

4. Kōa Shōken K.K. v. Yano, 14 Minshū 1169 (Sup. Ct., 3d Petty Bench, May 24, 1960). Securities exchanges as a rule prohibit members from effecting sales of listed securities outside the exchange market. *E.g.*, Tokyo Securities Exchange, Constitution, art. 23.

(5. See the footnote on next page)

Discretionary Accounts Exchange members are required to refrain from engaging in excessive transactions in their customers' discretionary accounts.[6] Since many of the disputes between securities companies and their customers have arisen over transactions in discretionary accounts, the authorities recently requested securities companies not to engage in such transactions except in accordance with strong demands on the part of their customers.[7] While the rule requires that a report on each contract of discretionary account be filed with the authorities,[8] the authorities as a matter of regulation suggests that securities companies have the customer surrender a written contract form with signature of the customer, including a clause to the effect that all profits and losses belong to him, and that companies file with the authority monthly reports on all transactions carried out by them in such accounts stating, among other items, the number of accounts which have gained profits and those which have suffered losses.[9]

Other Restrictions The Securities Exchange Law authorizes the Finance Minister to impose restrictions, by his rules, against transactions on the account of exchange members and transactions by those members in excessive amount,[10] but no such rules have been enacted thus far. The

---

5. Kawamoto, *Nomikōi no Igi* (Meaning of "swallowing"), SHŌJI HŌMU KENKYŪ (No. 209) 2 (1961).

With regard to the entrustment of transactions on the securities market, each member firm must act in accordance with the Entrustment Contract Rule (*jutaku keiyaku junsoku*) prescribed by the exchange to which he belongs. Items which must be stipulated therein are enumerated in SEL, art. 130 para. 2. The Finance Minister has administrative control over the contents of the Rule. SEL, art. 82 para. 2 item 1, art. 83 para. 1, art. 85–2 para. 1, and art. 156. The Rule constitutes an adhesive contract binding customers. *See* p. 7 *supra*.

6. SEL, art. 127; *Yūkashōken no Baibai-Ichininkanjō ni kansuru Kisoku* (Rule concerning discretionary accounts of securities), art. 1 (Securities Exchange Commission Rule No. 15, 1948).

7. Ministry of Finance Release (*zōri*) No. 926, Feb. 7, 1964. In accordance with this release, each association of securities firms prescribes in its rule that each member must prohibit its registered representatives from accepting discretionary orders from customers. *E.g.*, Tokyo Association of Securities Firms, Rule on Registered Representatives (Rule of Fair Practice No. 5), art. 9 para. 3 item 3; Osaka Association of Securities Firms, Rule on Registered Representatives (Rule of Fair Practice No. 6), art. 10 para. 3 item 4.

8. Rule concerning Discretionary Accounts of Securities (*supra* note 6), art. 2.

9. Ministry of Finance Release, *supra* note 7.

10. SEL, art. 127.

Minister is also authorized to issue a rule on a stop-loss order (*gyakusashine chūmon*),[11] one which has also yet to be enacted.[12]

2. Types of Transactions on Exchanges

Types of Transactions The time and methods of delivery of securities are stipulated by Business Regulations of exchanges.[13] Only four kinds of transactions are available on the exchange market: (1) cash delivery (*tōjitsu torihiki*); (2) regular way (*futsū torihiki*); (3) fortnightly settlement (*tokuyaku torihiki*); and (4) when-issued transaction (*hakkōbi torihiki*). The usual type of sale, as in the case of United States exchanges, is that of delivery regular way, and unless otherwise stated in the bid and offer, regular way is implied.[14]

When-Issued Transactions The when-issued transaction in Japan retains somewhat unique characteristics in that the sales period extends quite long (usually about a month) and that a liquidation by set-off through counter-sales is available without actual delivery.[15] For several years subsequent to World War II, future transactions in not-yet-issued stocks were considerably active on the over-the-counter market due to the strict regulation on tradings in issued stocks, representing a drastic change from the trading practice in pre-war times. Since this over-the-counter future transaction tended to be over-speculative, the authority had securities exchanges absorb and administer such transaction.[16] Today when-issued trading is available only for new shares of stock to be issued by corporations already in existence, but such transaction is still made mostly by speculators who lament the demise of the old future transaction.[17] A customer who entrusts a when-issued transaction must deposit with the securities company a certain

---

11. SEL, art. 133 item 2.

12. A stop-loss order may be freely made. SUZUKI & KAWAMOTO, 247–48.

13. SEL, art. 108. *E.g.*, Tokyo Securities Exchange, Business Regulations, art. 10 para. 1; Osaka Securities Exchange, Business Regulations, art. 10 para. 1.

14. *E.g.*, Tokyo Securities Exchange, Business Regulations, art. 10 para. 8; Osaka Securities Exchange, Business Regulations, art. 10 para. 7.

15. *Cf.* SEL, art. 49; Margin Transaction Rule, art. 1 para. 4.

16. Tatsuta, *Hakkōbi Torihiki no Kōzō* (Structure of a when-issued transaction), IMBESUTOMENTO, Mar.-Apr. 1962, at 2.

17. *See* p. 9 *supra*.

amount of bond (similar to the margin requirement), and the exchange member in turn is required to deposit such bond with the exchange.[18]

Short Sales There is also a restriction on short sales (*kara-uri*) of securities.[19] A rule similar to the SEC Rule 10a-1 requires that a sell order be marked either " long " or " short,"[20] but it prohibits only such short sales as effected below the price at which the last sale was made on the floor, without regard to the next preceding different price.[21] Moreover, in actual practice a sell order is not marked, since marking is no longer as necessary at present as it was in pre-war days when future transactions prevailed.[22]

3. Off-Floor Trading and Bulk Sales: Crossing

" *Baikai* " Securities exchanges prohibit generally their members from effecting sales in listed securities outside the exchange market. At the same time some exceptions to this prohibition are permitted, the most important of which is that for bulk sales.[23] In this connection it might be appropriate to refer to so-called *baikai* (a kind of " crossing "), which is not a real off-floor trading and is completely banned at present.

Baikai is a special term used only in securities and commodity industries. It refers to a way of effecting a transaction by matching a sell order with a buy order for the same security in the hands of a single exchange member (*tsukeawase baikai*), or by matching a customer's order with the member's own bid or offer (*shikiri baikai*), at the price at which the last sale of the security was executed on the exchange. So long as the sale contract on the exchange is concerned, the same member acts as both buyer and seller.

---

18. SEL, art. 49; Margin Transaction Rule, art. 3; Tokyo Securities Exchange, Business Regulations, art. 61–6; Osaka Securities Exchange, Business Regulations, art. 84–6.

19. SEL, art. 133 item 1.

20. *Yūkashōken no Kara-uri ni kansuru Kisoku* (Rule concerning short sale of securities), art. 1 (Securities Exchange Commission Rule No. 16, 1948).

21. Rule concerning Short Sale of Securities (*supra* note 20), art. 2 para. 1. Self-regulations of securities exchange follow the same principle: *E.g.*, Tokyo Securities Exchange, Business Regulations, art. 85; Osaka Securities Exchange, Business Regulations, art. 113.

22. Provisions on short sales are in practice ineffective. FUJITA 209; SUZUKI & KAWAMOTO 242.

23. Tokyo Securities Exchange, Constitution, art. 23; Osaka Securities Exchange, Constitution, art. 23.

Transactions by way of *baikai* have increased substantially in recent years.[24] Heated arguments have arisen lately in academic circles over how to explain the legality of this *baikai*, when a single member assumes both roles of the contract relationship and " swallowing " is prohibited. Although theories are quite varied, their conclusions are in agreement that *baikai* is legal and valid.[25] A district court has also held this opinion.[26] At times *baikai* has been abused and securities exchanges have had to cope with this problem.[27]

Ban of Baikai *Baikai* was completely abolished in October 1967. Its drawbacks, pointed out by many critics, can be classified as follows: (1) Since a single exchange member matches a selling order with a buying order for the same security, *baikai* prevents concentration of trading on the floor and hinders determination of the fair market price of the security. (2) *Baikai* is an exception to the principle of time priority (" first come, first served ") and deprives other members of an opportunity for favorable trading. (3) The customer's interests conflict with that of the members who execute the order according to the *shikiri baikai* method.[28]

To replace *baikai*, securities exchanges provide for the following two special procedures regarding block transactions.

Off-Floor Distribution of Listed Securities This procedure was introduced after the model of " Special Offering " provided by Rule 391 of the

---

24. In September 1967, *baikai* amounted to 42.1% of all transactions on exchange markets. The reasons for this are as follows: (1) the prohibition of " swallowing " (*nomikōi*); (2) the restriction on off-floor tradings; (3) bulk sales derived from securities investment trusts (mutual funds); (4) concentration of orders into the so-called " Big Four." FUJITA 197–200.

25. Ōsumi, *Shōkentorihikisho ni okeru iwayuru Baikai ni tsuite* (Concerning so-called *baikai* on securities exchange), 4 KEIZAIHŌ 2 (1961); Kawamoto, *supra* note 5; FUJITA 202.

26. Emori v. Sakamoto, HANREI JIHŌ (No. 217) 28 (Fukui Dist. Ct., Jan. 11, 1960). Under the old law, courts often held *baikai* valid. *E.g.*, Nishikawa v. Kishi, 23 Minroku 526 (Great Ct. of Cassation, Civil United Dept., Apr. 9, 1917).

27. In order to create a favorable " last sale price " at which *baikai* may be executed, some exchange members made a series of sales or purchases in the security. In February 1963 the Tokyo Securities Exchange, under the advice of the authorities, took the initiative in depressing such abuse by prohibiting members, as a rule, from effecting *baikai* at the last sale price which was formed by virtue of such members' participation. Tokyo Securities Exchange, Board of Directors Rule, Feb. 26, 1963. Other exchanges followed suit.

28. Tokyo Securities Exchange, 1968 *Shōken Nenkan* (Annual report on securities) 154; SUZUKI & KAWAMOTO 223.

New York Stock Exchange and came into force at the time of the abolishment of *baikai*. Where a customer's selling order of a block of securities exceeds the volume prescribed by the exchange,[29] and where it is difficult to execute the order on the floor in a reasonable time and at a reasonable price or prices, the member, with prior approval of the customer as to charging a special fee in addition to the usual commission, may execute the order through off-floor distribution.[30] The member must obtain prior approval of the securities exchange during the trading hours and the transaction shall be executed within the next business day.[31] The exchange shall announce the terms of the off-floor distribution after the closing of floor trading of the day on which it gave approval.[32] The off-floor distribution shall be executed in either of the following two ways : (a) by matching buying orders with the offering at a price fixed by the customer ranging between the closing price of the day when the exchange gave the approval and 95 percent of that price, or (b) by auction in which bids shall exceed 95 percent of the closing price of the day when the exchange gave the approval.[33]

Block Sales and Block Purchases on the Floor These procedures were introduced along the lines of " Exchange Distributions and Exchange Acquisitions " provided by Rule 392 of the New York Stock Exchange and came into force in February 1968. Where a customer's order to sell or to purchase a block of securities in the regular way exceeds the volume prescribed by the exchange, and where it is difficult to execute the order in a reasonable time and at a reasonable price or prices, the member, on the condition that he charge the customer an entrustment commission at a special rate, may solicit from others who are off the floor the purchase of the security in the case of block sale, or solicit from others off the floor the sale of the security in the case of block purchase and may execute the order through auction on the floor. With prior approval of the customer, the

29. Minimum volume ranges from fifty thousand to three million shares depending upon the average trading volume during the preceding six months. Tokyo Securities Exchange, Rule concerning Off-Floor Distribution, art. 1.

30. Tokyo Securities Exchange, Business Regulations, art. 89 para. 1 ; Osaka Securities Exchange, Business Regulations, art. 117 para. 1.

31. Tokyo Securities Exchange, Business Regulations, art. 89 para. 2 ; Osaka Securities Exchange, Business Regulations, art. 117 para. 2.

32. Tokyo Securities Exchange, Business Regulations, art. 89 para. 3 ; Osaka Securities Exchange, Business Regulations, art. 117 para 3.

33. Tokyo Securities Exchange, Business Regulations, arts. 89–2 and 90 ; Osaka Securities Exchange, Business Regulations, arts. 117–2 and 118.

member may, in addition to the entrustment commission above mentioned, collect a special fee for the block sale or block purchase which is prescribed by the exchange.[34] The member must obtain the prior approval of the securities exchange and must file a report with the securities exchange after completion of such transaction pursuant to the rule prescribed by the securities exchange.[35]

Crossing In addition to the foregoing methods, available also are those of "crossing" of customers' order and "crossing" for the account of the member firm itself. A major difference from the *baikai* is that before the firm makes a crossing the member must cry on the floor an asked price which is higher than the firm's bid price by the minimum trading fluctuation. In other words, a cross is effected in an open way and constitutes part of floor trading.[36]

4. Transfer of Stock

How to Transfer A bearer form stock certificate is uncommon, perhaps nonexistent, in Japan, although it is legitimate. Stock of register form used to be transferred by means of endorsement consisting of either a signature or a combination of the transferor's name and his seal. The name could be handwritten (even by others), typewritten or printed, and the seal did not have to coincide with that which had been filed with the corporation. Frequently endorsements were made even by seals only, without transferor's names. Thus endorsement turned into an empty formality and failed to function as a safeguard for the shareowner. The 1966 amendment completely abolished endorsement on stock certificates, and made even register form stock transferable by mere delivery of certificates.[37]

Stock without Certificate This was a drastic change and some share-

---

34. Tokyo Securities Exchange, Business Regulations, art. 29 para. 1 and art. 30; Osaka Securities Exchange, Business Regulations, art. 29 para. 1 and art. 30.

35. Tokyo Securities Exchange, Business Regulations, art. 29 paras. 2 and 3, and art. 30; Osaka Securities Exchange, Business Regulations, art. 29 paras. 2 and 3, and art. 30.

36. SUZUKI & KAWAMOTO 224–25. The volume of crossings is less than half of that of *baikai*. Between October 1968 and March 1969, the volume of crossings amounted to 15.9% of the total trading volume of the Tokyo Securities Exchange, floor section I. 1969 MOF ANN. REP. 5.

37. COMM. CODE, art. 205. This device seems to be quite unique to Japan.

holders may well feel uneasy about holding stock certificates. In order to appease those who opposed the abolishment of endorsement the legislature introduced a somewhat unique system. A shareholder who does not want to keep certificates of register form stock may request the corporation to that effect, and the corporation is required to state the fact in the shareholder register or to deposit such certificates with a bank or trust company.[38] Since a transfer of stock must be made by delivery of the certificate, the shareholder may at any time request the corporation to issue or return the certificate.[39] This is a rather complicated practice and a corporation may dispense with this obligation by an express provision in its charter.[40]

Shareholder Register The transferee may not lay claim against the corporation that he is entitled to the rights of a shareholder until his name and address have been inscribed in the shareholder register.[41] A corporation may employ transfer agents and registrars;[42] transfer agents are very popular at present, whereas registrars are nonexistent in Japan. Securities exchanges now require issuer corporations to maintain transfer agents.[43] A corporation may close the shareholder register for a period of not more than two months prior to the date of a shareholders' meeting or the date when shareholders exercise their rights.[44]

Lost or Stolen Shares As a share of stock may be transferred by means of mere delivery of the certificate, a possessor of a stock certificate is presumed to be a legitimate bearer thereof.[45] Where a person has, in any manner whatsoever, been dispossessed of a stock certificate, the new possessor of the certificate is not obligated to return the certificate unless he has acquired it in bad faith, or unless in acquiring it he has been guilty of gross negligence.[46]

---

38. COMM. CODE, art. 226–2 paras. 1 and 2. The stock certificate surrendered to the corporation upon such request is to be canceled. COMM. CODE, art. 226–2, para. 3.

39. COMM. CODE, art. 226–2 para. 4.

40. COMM. CODE, art. 226–2 para. 1.

41. COMM. CODE, art. 206 para. 1.

42. COMM. CODE, art. 206 paras. 2 and 3.

43. *E.g.*, Tokyo Securities Exchange, Listing Standards for Stock, art. 4 para. 1 item 7; Osaka Securities Exchange, Listing Standards for Stock, art. 4 para. 1 item 7.

44. COMM. CODE, art. 224–3 paras. 1 and 2.

45. COMM. CODE, art. 205 para. 2.

46. COMM. CODE, art. 229; *Kogittehō* (Law on checks), art. 21 (Law No. 57, 1933).

A stock certificate may be declared void by a judgment of nullification therefor subsequent to a public peremptory notice.[47]

According to the majority view, when a new stock certificate is issued by the corporation, the certificate becomes effective at the moment when it enters into the shareholder's possession. Therefore a certificate while being mailed by the corporation to the shareholder is nothing but an invalid piece of paper, although such certificate is usually covered by transportation insurance.

47. Comm. Code, art. 230; Civil Procedure Code, arts. 764 through 785 (Law No. 29, 1890).

Chapter 12

Credit Extension in Connection with Securities Transactions

1. Restriction in Case of Distribution

A securities company which has been an underwriter and is seeking to sell the underwritten security is prohibited from extending credit to the purchaser of the security prior to six months after the date on which the company became an underwriter.[1] Although this restriction may have been introduced for the purpose of achieving segregation between underwriting and broker activities,[2] it has seldom been discussed in Japan. This may be either because the restriction has been neglected or because credit on securities is not so well supplied as to necessitate restriction in Japan.[3]

2. Margin Transactions

Scope of Credit Control The Securities Exchange Law regulates credit extension less broadly than the U. S. law, controlling credit extended by securities companies only, and only in connection with a special type of transaction, i.e., margin transaction (*shin'yō torihiki*).[4] Neither credit extension by persons other than a securities company nor borrowing by securities companies is regulated, on the grounds that in Japan there is no danger of excessive credit extension in connection with securities.[5]

---

1. SEL, art. 61.

2. Securities Exchange Act of 1934, sec. 11 (d), 15 U.S.C.A. § 78k (d); 2 Loss, Securities Regulation 684 (2d ed. 1961).

3. Suzuki & Kawamoto 63.

4. SEL, art. 49; Margin Transaction Rule. In other words, there is no regulation corresponding to section 7 (d), Regulation U thereunder, and section 8 of the Securities Exchange Act of 1934. On the other hand, the Japanese regulation is broader than the U.S. one in that the Margin Transaction Rule covers also when-issued transactions.

5. Credit extension is even encouraged by means of securities finance companies. *See* p. 100 *infra*.

Purpose and Method of Regulation Margin transactions are regulated in order to prevent excessive market fluctuations.[6] The Finance Minister is authorized to prescribe rules on margin transactions.[7] In exact reversal to the American system of regulation, the Minister fixes the margin rate, which may not be below thirty percent of the value of the securities concerned.[8] Deposit may be made in the form of collateral securities, the permissible loan value of which is fixed by ministerial rule.[9] Details are stipulated in the rules of securities exchanges.[10]

Loan Transactions One of the characteristics of Japanese margin transaction is that it is related to a loan transaction (*taishaku torihiki*) whereby a member firm borrows money and/or securities from a securities finance company. A securities company has only to borrow the balance between the sale and purchase orders within the same brand. The securities finance company loans money or securities through the clearing department of the

---

6. In the United States, three purposes are enumerated: (1) prevention of excessive use of credit by the securities industry; (2) protection of margin purchasers; and (3) prevention of excessive market fluctuation. 2 Loss, Securities Regulation 1242 (2d ed. 1961).

7. SEL, art. 49. The board of governors of the Bank of Japan is supposed to have the power to control credit extension in connection with securities. *Nippon Ginkō-hō* (Law on the Bank of Japan), art. 13–3 item 7. However, this provision has been inactive, and no rules thereunder have been formulated.

8. SEL, art. 49 para. 1. Here again, behind the provision lies the fact that the securities market in Japan is not so closely connected with the finance market as in the United States. Oda, Miwa & Sumi 102; Suzuki & Kawamoto 271.

9. SEL, art. 49 para. 2; Margin Transaction Rule, art. 5.

10. *E.g.*, The Tokyo Securities Exchange Entrustment Contract Rules provide as follows. In order for a customer to make a margin transaction he must have a margin account with a member firm, submitting a certificate stipulating the opening of a margin account (art. 12). Even where a customer has a margin account with the securities company, his order is considered a spot transaction unless he specifically designates it as a margin transaction (art. 13). The customer must deposit with the securities company as a margin thirty percent of the contract price (150,000 yen is minimum) by noon of the following day (art. 13–2). The securities company extends the loan to the customer in money or securities on the day when the transaction is liquidated as a regular way trading on the exchange (art. 13–3 paras. 1 and 3). The loan falls due on the following day, but it is automatically deferred, for a maximum period of six months, unless notice is given three days before the date when the customer plans to liquidate (art. 13–5). Most margin transactions are liquidated through offset. Suzuki & Kawamoto 265. Where the customer fails to meet his obligations the securities company may liquidate through offset on the customer's account, as well as request damages (art. 13–9).

securities exchange. The securities company must deposit with the securities finance company thirty percent of the money or of the value of shares borrowed as a bond. The borrower may liquidate the loan transaction either through offset or through actual delivery, again via the clearing department of the securities exchange.[11]

Recent Reforms The Securities Counseling Commission in its report of September 14, 1966, pointed out certain items to be improved with regard to margin transactions.[12] Along this line reforms were made in 1967. The number of brands available for loan transactions was considerably increased. The minimum amount of margin was fixed in order to discourage transaction by indigent investors. The deferrable period was extended from three months to six months in order to mitigate the pressure of the liquidation date. In addition, measures were taken to lighten customers' burdens.[13]

3. Securities Finance Companies

Provisions regarding a securities finance company (*shōkenkin'yū-gaisha*) were added to the Securities Exchange Law by the 1950 amendment.[14] At present three such companies exist in Japan: Nippon Securities Finance Company, Osaka Securities Finance Company, and Chūbu Securities Finance Company.

Business and Control The purpose of a securities finance company is "to engage in the business of lending money and securities necessary for liquidation of margin transactions to members of a securities exchange, through a clearing system of the securities exchange concerned."[15] In this connection, the law requires that such company be a stock corporation with fifty million yen or more stated capital.[16] Furthermore, the company must obtain a business license from the Finance Minister, and the law prescribes the application form, the requirements for license and other

---

11. SUZUKI & KAWAMOTO 267.
12. 1968 MOF ANN. REP. 255.
13. 1968 MOF ANN. REP. 14–15; 1969 MOF ANN. REP. 6.
14. SEL, Chapter 5–2 (arts. 156–2 through 156–14). Forerunners of securities finance companies may be found in pre-war days. SUZUKI & KAWAMOTO 259.
15. SEL, art. 156–3 para. 1.
16. SEL, art. 156–2.

procedures.[17] Finally, the Finance Minister has broad and strong regulatory power over securities finance companies including the power to revoke the license and to order suspension of business within a six-month period.[18]

Raison d'Être After World War II, Japanese banks were unable to lend money for margin transactions because their funds were insufficient and they had to lend a huge amount of money to industrial corporations. Furthermore, there was no system through which member firms could borrow securities.[19] Under such circumstances it was necessary to establish securities finance companies which would lend money and securities for margin transactions to member firms. Securities finance companies raise funds for loan mainly from call-money brokers, who in turn raise their funds from the Bank of Japan. The Bank of Japan and the Ministry of Finance, therefore, can easily control the amount of money which is to be used for margin transactions and thus they can also control excessive speculation on the stock market.[20]

---

17. SEL, arts. 156–3 through 156–5.

18. SEL, arts. 156–6 through 156–14.

19. In the case of time-transactions which were predominant in pre-war days, settlement was postponed until the liquidation date. In other words, the buyer and seller extended credit to each other. The parties made a counter-transaction on or by that date and settled the transaction by paying and receiving the balance. Therefore they did not need to borrow money or securities from third parties. However, the so-called " Three Principles on Securities Transactions " (p. 11 note 28 *supra*) required, as a condition for reopening securities exchanges, that time-transactions be banned. In the case of margin transactions, common in the United States, the transaction on the floor is a spot-transaction (regular way) and credit is extended to the buyer or seller by the broker. Margin transactions, therefore, presuppose an organized money-lending market and securities-lending market. SUZUKI & KAWAMOTO 257–58.

20. SUZUKI & KAWAMOTO 258–60.

CHAPTER 13

Securities Investment Trust

1. Types of Investment Trust

Definition A securities investment trust (*shōken tōshishintaku*) is statutorily defined as " a trust for the purpose of operating the trust fund as an investment in specified securities under the direction of a manager company, and for the purpose of having unspecified many persons acquire fractions of its beneficiary rights."[1]

Under present law, such a body is required to take the form of " trust," as stipulated in a special statute.[2] It follows that only a contractual type is available in Japan. A corporation type of investment trust, such as mutual funds in the United States, has not yet been recognized in Japan, despite efforts in the past. This lack of recognition is due mainly to rigid control of corporation law.[3]

Unit Investment Trust Approximately two-thirds of all investment trusts take the form of a unit investment trust (*tan'igata tōshishintaku*).[4] A unit trust is operated for a period of seven years.[5] The principal of a trust fund is not increased during the period of operation of a unit trust. On the other hand, a trust certificate may be repurchased and the investment con-

---

1. SITL, art. 2 para. 1. *Kashitsukeshintakuhō* (Loan trust law) (Law No. 195, 1952) is a sister statute of the SITL.

2. *Shintakuhō* (Trust law) (Law No. 62, 1922). The SITL contains several modifications to the Trust Law.

3. Bills of 1948 and 1954 contained provisions on investment companies. Obstacles in corporation law include: (1) prohibition from acquiring the corporation's own stock (p. 15 *supra*); (2) requirement to hold shareholder meeting, difficult to fulfill where bearer form shares are issued. Recently, the feasibility of introducing the corporation type of investment trust has been undergoing reexamination.

4. In 1968 newly formed unit investment trusts totaled 150.8 billion yen, whereas open investment trusts amounted to 81.1 billion yen. 1969 MOF ANN. REP. 111.

5. At the outset the trust period was two years. It was extended to three years in 1953, five years in 1956 and seven years in 1966.

tract may be cancelled. In this sense a unit investment trust is actually nothing but a kind of open-end trust. Accordingly it is often called a semi-open or semi-closed trust.

Open Investment Trust Its only alternative is an open investment trust (*tsuikagata tōshishintaku*), comparable to the British flexible trust of cash fund method. Additional trust funds may be created and the investment contract may be cancelled. A trust lasts indefinitely, subject to certain resolutive conditions.[6] Investment trusts in debt securities take this form.

Constructive Investment Trust The 1967 amendment to the Securities Investment Trust Law introduced a new concept of constructive investment trust (*minashi tōshishintaku*). This is a trust for the purpose of having the trustee acquire beneficiary rights.[7] Operating each unit trust independently is cumbersome and expensive. The device of constructive investment trust makes it possible to integrate multiple units under single direction.[8]

2. Parties to an Investment Trust

Manager Company It is the manager company (*itaku-gaisha*) that issues directions with regard to the operation of trust funds. A manager company must be a stock corporation with not less than fifty million yen stated capital,[9] and must be licensed by the Finance Minister.[10] The Minister also has broad supervisory powers over such a company.[11]

Formerly securities companies acted as manager companies. As of April 1, 1960, however, the " Big Four " attained segregation of the manager business, and other securities companies followed suit.[12] At the same

6. Prior to the 1956 amendment, the trust period was limited to ten years.

7. SITL, art. 2–2.

8. Tanaka, Family Fund *ni tsuite* (On family funds), Shōji Hōmu Kenkyū (No. 534) 13–15 (1970). In this sense it resembles a " fund of funds " and is commonly called a " mother fund."

9. SITL, art. 4 para. 2.

10. SITL, art. 6 para. 1. Procedures and standards for license are similar to those for licensing of a securities company. SITL, art. 6 paras. 2 and 3, arts. 7 and 8.

11. SITL, arts. 9 through 15, 18, 18–3 through 24.

12. In March 1959 debate was held in the Diet as to the legality of securities companies' managerial activities, in the light of protection of investors and Civil Code article 108 prohibiting a person from acting as an agent of both parties to a contract.

After segregation, independence of manager companies from their parents was gradually achieved in terms of shareholdings.

time the " Big Four " formed their subsidiaries for the purpose of distributing trust certificates.

Trustee Company A trustee company (*jutaku-gaisha*) must be a trust company or a trust bank. As a point of fact, all trustee companies are trust banks.[13]

Certificate Holder A person becomes a beneficiary (*juekisha*) of a securities investment trust by acquiring a trust certificate (*juekishōken*).[14] A trust certificate is a security within the meaning of the Securities Exchange Law,[15] but it is exempt from the registration requirement.[16] Accordingly, a prospectus need not accompany a sale of trust certificates. The law requires that the manager company furnish a statement on the trust certificate, a sort of quasi-prospectus.[17]

3. Investment Trust Deed

Role of a Deed A trust contract (*shintaku keiyaku*) between a manager company and a trustee company has to be based upon an investment trust deed (*shintaku yakkan*) approved by the Finance Minister in advance.[18] In this sense an investment trust deed is a prototype of a trust contract. Since it provides the basis of legal relationships among parties to an investment trust, approval by the Finance Minister is required for the original deed as well as for amendments thereto.[19]

---

13. A trust company must be a stock corporation with stated capital of not less than one million yen, and must be licensed by the minister concerned. *Shintakugyōhō* (Trust business law), art. 1 para. 1, art. 2 (Law No. 65, 1922). In order for a commercial bank to engage in the trust business, it must obtain a license from the Finance Minister. Law No. 43, 1943, art. 1.

14. SITL, art. 5 para. 2. A trust certificate is of bearer form unless the holder requests otherwise. SITL, art. 5 para. 4.

15. SEL, art. 2 para. 1 item 7.

16. SEL, art. 3 para. 1.

17. SITL, art. 20–2 para. 1; SITL Enforcement Rule, art. 11 (Ministry of Finance Rule No. 68, 1953). Provisions are datailed in Ministry of Finance Release (*zōshō*) No. 695, Apr. 1, 1968.

18. SITL, art. 12 para. 1. The term *yakkan* generally means an adhesive contract clause, but *shintaku yakkan* does not have such connotation.

19. SITL, arts. 13 and 14. Items to be stated in an investment trust deed are as follows: (1) identity of the manager company and the trustee company; (2) matters concerning beneficiaries; (3) businesses of the manager company and the trustee company;

Operation of Trust Fund One of the most important items of a trust deed is that concerning the operation of a trust fund. A manager company has the duty of loyalty in issuing directions regarding the operation of such a fund.[20] A manager company may not order the trustee company to deal with the manager company, or its directors or ten percent shareholders, nor to engage in transactions among the trust funds under its common direction.[21] Limits are stipulated with regard to the maximum percentage of the total in issue of any one security to be held by the trust funds under the common direction of the manager company.[22]

Legal Nature of a Deed The Securities Investment Trust Law focuses on the trust contract between a manager company and a trustee company. Trust certificate holders are not prominent in the law. In reality, however, investment trust deeds do contain provisions concerning a manager company's duty vis-à-vis certificate holders. Prevailing view is that an investment trust deed should confine itself to the legal relationship between a manager company and a trustee company, and that the legal relationship between certificate holders and the manager company should be stipulated in another deed.[23] On the other hand, the view has been expressed that

(4) amount of the principal trusted; (5) matters concerning trust certificates; (6) matters concerning management and operation of the principal trusted and of the income therefrom; (7) matters concerning redemption of the principal trusted and distribution of dividends; (8) period of the trust contract, extension and cancellation thereof; (9) accounting periods for the trust; (10) method of calculation, time and means of payment, of manager's and trustee's charges and other fees; (11) amendment to the trust deed; (12) matters concerning transfer of all or a part of the manager company's business; (13) matters concerning resignation of the manager company and appointment of the incoming manager company. SITL, art. 12 para. 2; SITL Enforcement Rule, art. 5.

20. SITL, art. 17 para. 1.

21. SITL, art. 17 para. 2 items 1 and 2.

22. Shares of stock and unsecured debentures, 10%; national and local government bonds, bonds guaranteed by the government, notes issued by a corporation pursuant to a special statute, and secured corporate debentures, 30%; trust certificates of a constructive investment trust, 100%. SITL, art. 17 para. 2 item 3; *Shōken tōshishintaku no Itakugaisha no Kōijunsoku ni kansuru Shōrei* (Ministerial rule concerning practice norms of a manager company of a securities investment trust), art. 2 (Ministry of Finance Rule No. 60, 1967). The maximum percentage of trust funds to be invested in any one security is stipulated in the investment trust deed. A ten percent rule is operative here.

23. Watanabe, *Hōritsumen kara mita Shōken Tōshishintaku no Mondaiten* (Legal problems of a securities investment trust), 33 (2) HŌRITSU JIHŌ 34 (1961); Yukihira, *Shōken Tōshishintaku Yakkan no Seikaku* (Nature of a securities investment trust deed), SHŌJI HŌMU KENKYŪ (No. 204) 141 (1961).

an investment trust deed should be regarded as general contract clauses, stipulating the legal relationship not only between a manager company and a trustee company but also among all parties to a securities investment trust, and consequently comparable to the charter of a corporation.[24]

24. Suzuki, *Shōken Tōshishintaku Yakkan no Hōtekiseishitsu* (Legal nature of a securities investment trust deed), 4 KEIZAIHŌ 17 (1961).

CHAPTER 14

International Aspect of Securities Transactions

1. Foreign Securities

Restrictions In connection with the liberalization code, Japan made a complete reservation on direct investment abroad by residents and a limited reservation on purchase abroad, by residents, of listed securities.[1] A permit from the Finance Minister must be obtained in order for a resident to subscribe for or acquire a foreign security.[2] Recently the government has established a policy to remove these restrictions by degrees.[3]

---

1. OECD, CODE OF LIBERALISATION OF CAPITAL MOVEMENTS, 99–101 (1969).

2. *Gaikokukawase oyobi Gaikokubōeki Kanrihō* (Foreign exchange and foreign trade control law), art. 32, art. 35 item 1 (Law No. 228, 1949); *Gaikokukawase Kanrirei* (Foreign exchange control rule), art. 14 (Cabinet Rule No. 203, 1950). Where a transaction of fifty thousand dollars or less meets certain conditions, such as serving to improve the national balance of payments, the authority to issue a permit is delegated to the Bank of Japan.

3. On July 15, 1969, the Ministry of Finance presented its policy on liberalizing direct investment abroad before the general assembly of the Foreign Capital Counseling Committee. In the case of an investment in a foreign corporation in which a Japanese party or parties holds twenty-five percent or more equity shares and maintains an office with one or more full-time officers: (1) investment abroad of 200,000 dollars or less will be automatically validated; (2) investment abroad exceeding 200,000 dollars but less than 300,000 dollars will be examined by the Bank of Japan, and under less stringent standards. Purchase of foreign shares through the market is excluded from the foregoing liberalization plan. Also excluded are investments in such industry or area as will do harm to financial institutions or the national economy of Japan, and investments in non-member countries of the International Monetary Fund. SHŌMURA, *Shihon Jiyūka to Shōkenshijō* (Liberalization of capital movement and the securities market) 77–78 (1969).

In April 1970 the Ministry of Finance granted validation and approval necessary for Japanese securities investment trusts to acquire foreign securities in their portfolio. At present only four manager companies, affiliated with the "Big Four," are qualified to engage in this business. Assets represented by foreign currencies, including foreign securities, may not exceed thirty percent of the net asset value of each trust fund. For the time being, investment trusts may purchase stock and debentures listed on the exchanges of New York, London, Paris, Frankfurt, Amsterdam, Sidney, Zurich and Toronto. Short-term government bonds may be purchased even though they are not listed. Stock in investment companies are excluded. *See* Fujita, *Tōshishintaku no Gaikokushōken Kumiire* (Purchase of foreign securities by investment trusts), SHŌJI HŌMU KENKYŪ (No. 524) 11–15 (1970).

Japanese Regulation Apart from the above restrictions, foreign securities may be traded like domestic ones. The scope of securities within the meaning of the Securities Exchange Law is the same both in cases of foreign and domestic issuers.[4] Stock certificates, subscription warrants and corporate debentures issued by foreign corporations and trust certificates of foreign securities investment trusts and foreign loan trusts are subject to the registration requirement and the statutory prospectus requirement where they are sold by means of a public offering or secondary distribution.[5]

2. Foreign Investors

Restrictions A reservation is made on direct investment in Japan by nonresidents and on purchase by nonresidents of listed shares or other securities of a participating nature which would have the effect of: (1) increasing above seven percent participation by a single foreign investor in the stated capital of an individual enterprise; (2) increasing above fifteen percent the total foreign participation in the stated capital of an individual enterprise in a restricted industry; or (3) increasing above twenty percent total foreign participation in the stated capital of an individual enterprise in a non-restricted industry.[6]

In order for a foreign investor to acquire securities issued by an existing Japanese corporation, he must obtain validation from the minister concerned.[7] Within the foregoing limits, however, validation is automatically conferred by the Bank of Japan.

Japanese Securities Abroad It is prohibited for any person to issue or publicly offer abroad a security payable in Japanese currency, or for a resident to issue or publicly offer a security abroad unless such has been vali-

---

4. SEL, art. 2 para. 1 item 8.

5. SEL, art. 3 para. 2; Registration Rule, art. 3 item 1.

6. OECD, *supra* note 1, at 97–99. With regard to direct investment, if certain requirements are met, the limits may be exceeded and foreign participation may amount to as much as fifty percent in Class 1 liberalized industries and one hundred percent in Class 2 liberalized industries. The number of such industries is increasing.

7. *Gaishi ni kansuru Hōritsu* (Law concerning foreign investment), arts. 11 (Law No. 163, 1950); Cabinet Rule No. 221, 1952, art. 4; Foreign Exchange and Foreign Trade Control Law, art. 35 item 2; Foreign Exchange Control Rule, art. 14. SHŌMURA, *supra* note 3, at 27, provides convenient table explaining when a validation is necessary.

dated.[8] A considerable number of brands—national and local government bonds, corporate debentures and shares of stock—have been issued in the United States and Europe.[9] In addition, securities have been purchased by foreign investors irrespective of the issuer's intent.[10]

Where a Japanese security is traded within United States territory, extraterritorial application of U. S. law to the Japanese issuer comes into question. The SEC of the United States takes the position that the 12(g) registration is applicable to such issuers.[11] American shareholders are often deprived of their right to subscribe to additional shares because their standing proxy refuses to subscribe them on their account, lacking registration with the SEC, in fear of violating section 5 of the 1933 Act.[12]

3. Foreign Securities Firms

The securities industry has not been liberalized yet, although liberalization is only a matter of time. Securities exchanges confine their membership to domestic firms.[13] It is reported that the Ministry of Finance is considering the enactment of a special statute regulating foreign securities firms, especially their establishment of branch offices in Japan.[14] The content of such regulation is not yet concretely fixed. Apart from this coming legislation, foreign securities firms would be subject to following regulation.

---

8. Foreign Exchange and Foreign Trade Control Law, art. 34 items 1 and 2.

9. Shares of stock take the form of ADR (American Depositary Receipts), EDR (European Depositary Receipts), LDR (London Depositary Receipts) or CDR (Curaçao Depositary Receipts).

10. Several investment trusts formed abroad have purchased Japanese securities. 1969 MOF ANN. REP. 62–65.

11. SECURITIES EXCHANGE ACT OF 1934, sec. 12(g), 15 U.S.C.A. § 78 *l*(g); Rule 12g3-2(a) and Rule 12g3-2(b)(1), 17 C.F.R. §§ 240. 12g3-2(a), 240. 12g3-2(b) (1). Some corporations file with the SEC periodic reports and other documents. Several corporations filed registration statement with the SEC when they issued ADRs, for this reason they file annual reports pursuant to section 15(d) of the Securities Exchange Act of 1934. *See also* California Corporate Securities Law of 1968, §§ 25130, 25101.

12. The standing proxy sells the subscription warrant or otherwise according to the instruction given by the principal.

13. *See* p. 83 note 15 *supra*. Similar discrimination is made by the New York Stock Exchange. NYSE, Constitution, Article IX, section 2.

14. *The Nihon Kōgyō Shimbun* (Japan Industrial Journal), May 29, 1970, p. 2; *The Nippon Keizai Shimbun*, June 25, 1970, p. 1.

Before doing business in Japan, a foreign corporation is required to appoint its representative in Japan, to set up an office within Japanese territory, and to register its representative and office in the commerical registry.[15] A securities company must be a licensed stock corporation.[16] A foreign corporation is classified according to its closest Japanese counterpart[17]. Unless a foreign securities firm establishes a subsidiary in the form of a stock corporation pursuant to Japanese law, it must be a corporate body equivalent to a Japanese stock corporation in order to be eligible to apply for a license with the Finance Minister.[18]

15. COMM. CODE, arts. 479 and 481.

16. SEL, art. 28.

17. COMM. CODE, art. 485–2. Types of business corporations are stock corporations (*kabushiki-gaisha*), partnership corporations (*gōmei-gaisha*), limited partnership corporations (*gōshi-gaisha*) and limited liability corporations (*yūgen-gaisha*). COMM. CODE, art. 53 ; *Yūgengaishahō* (Limited liability corporation law), art. 89 (Law No. 74, 1938).

18. An equivalent type would be the following : stock corporation, company limited by shares, *Aktiengesellschaft*, *société anonyme*, *società per azioni*.

Postscript: Reform Project

Pre-war securities regulation was a European system grafted onto traditional Japanese practices. Post-war legislation began as a carbon copy of the U. S. securities acts. Subsequent amendments have represented, in a sense, a reaction to achieve better harmony with Japanese society.

At the present stage, when the Securities Exchange Law is more than twenty years old and the securities industry shows considerable growth, an overhaul of the law merits consideration to meet the needs of a new era. The Securities Counseling Commission set up an expert subcommittee in May 1969 to examine possible amendments.[1]

It is expected that the subcommittee will scrutinize the following points:[2] (1) the disclosure system, especially improvement of continuous disclosure in the trading market;[3] (2) segregation of broker and dealer activities, especially in connecton with cross transactions and article 47 of the Law;[4] (3) manipulation and stabilization, to make the provisions thereon workable and effective; (4) unfair practices, especially legislative measures to cope with insider tradings;[5] (5) regulation of investment advisers; and (6) adjustments necessary to face internationalization of securities transactions, such as regulation of foreign securities, foreign broker-dealer-underwriters, foreign investment companies and tender offers.

---

1. Members of the subcommittee are Takeo Suzuki (chairman), Professor Emeritus, University of Tokyo, and member of the Securities Counseling Commission; Makoto Yazawa, Professor, University of Tokyo; Ichirō Kawamoto, Professor, Kobe University; and Takashi Hoshino, Managing Director, Tokyo Securities Exchange.

2. Sakano, *Shōkentorihikihō no Mondaiten to sono Haikei* (Problems of the Securities Exchange Law and their background), SHŌJI HŌMU KENKYŪ (No. 487) 5–6 (1969).

3. *See* p. 55 *supra*. False or misleading representations in a registration statement incurs strict civil liability (SEL, arts. 18 and 20), whereas there is no comparable provision regarding a periodic report. *Cf.* COMM. CODE, art. 266–3.

4. *See* p. 95 *supra*.

5. Short-swing profits derived from insider tradings must be disgorged. SEL, art. 189. Insiders' duty to notify the Ministry of Finance as to the change in their holdings was repealed by the 1953 amendment, making it difficult to invoke article 189. Yazawa, The Legal Structure for Corporate Enterprise: Shareholder-Management Relations under Japanese Law, in LAW IN JAPAN 547, 557 (VON MEHREN ED. 1963). Moreover, article 58 of the Securities Exchange Law does not function like U.S. Rule 10b-5, despite the similarity in wording.

Securities regulation is one of the fields where international unification is possible. May it be realized, not by the force of economic superiority of a predominant country, but by virtue of mutual understanding among all people and recognition of the merits in foreign laws and legal practices.

INDEX

This table is designed to serve as a glossary as well. References are to pages.

C

G

H

K

L

M

N

O

P

Q

R

S

U

V

W

Y

Z